THE GREAT ETERNAL TRUTHS

P.E. Bedell   **&**   **Theo Vaes**

Senior Research Scientist (Retd)   Researcher Global Problems

I C F R E (INDIA)   FREE LANCE (BELGIUM)

Contents

Preface

This is a book meant for popular reading. But it introduces the Reader to topics which could be used as study material when included in a Text Book of General Science, for a better understanding of our life on this earth and its long term objective, and the process by which the objective is achieved.

These topics are (1) Gravity (2) Electromagnetism (3) Thermodynamics (4) Newtons Laws of Motion (5) Application of Planck's Quantum Theory to Biological Reactions (6) Mendelian Genetics Population Genetics Molecular Genetics (7) Paleontology, Paleo Climatology, Paleo Magnetism. (8) Evolution of Life-forms and Its Objective (9) Practical Application of Einstein's Theory of Relativity.

These topics could be taken up for study by undergraduates or students passing out of school for a better understanding of life with its various experiences

About The Authors

P.E.Bedell (Prema Edwina Bedell) is a Research Scientist who began her career in the Forest Research Institute in Dehradun India in1961 in her maiden name of P.G.Pattanath (Prema Gopalan Pattanath) to work on the taxonomy of Bamboos. After that she has worked on a number of national level and international projects such as the FAO project of DANIDA known as Indo Danish Project on Seed Procurement and Tree Improvement. After the completion of the Project she was transferred to Coimbatore as Head of the Department of Seed Science and Technology, of the Institute of Forest Genetics and Tree Breeding– a branch of ICFRE. During her career she has participated in a number of Forestry Conferences, symposiums, and workshops and has 45 research papers to her credit mostly in her maiden name of P.G Pattanath. After her marriage her name was changed to P.E.Bedell (Prema Edwina Bedell). From then on, her publications are in the name of P.E.Bedell. She took voluntary retirement in 1992 and spent her retirement period in writing some text books in Forestry. She has published three books (1)Taxonomy of Bamboos published by APC Publishers New Delhi 1997. (2) Seed Science and Technology of Indian Forestry Species published by Allied Publishers Ltd New Delhi 1998. (3) Tree Breeding for Genetic Improvement of Tropical Tree Species published by Allied Publishers Ltd New Delhi 2006. All of these are still being sold on the internet.

Theo Vaes is a Business Entrepreneur and a Social Activist by profession. He has a wide range of interests and is a prolific reader. He attempts to find new applications for different scientific inventions and so increase their marketability and improve trade. During his market research he has travelled widely all over Europe, Africa, and Asia and has taken the opportunity to study the influence of customs and culture on attitudes and values of life of different communities. He is the President of the Governing Board of a number of social welfare organizations both in his own country of Belgium and abroad. In India, for a number of years he has been the President of the Governing Board of the VRO (India) a branch of an international social welfare organization, the objective of which is to train, educate, and empower, marginalized village people to bring them into the mainstream of life. In Belgium, he has drawn up a program called ATK in Dutch, the objective of which is to eliminate endemic poverty by a unique method of bringing the rich and the poor together, and training them and motivating them to change their attitudes towards each other, to work for each other instead of exploiting each other. This has the potential of becoming a world wide movement for bringing down poverty, crime, and thus controlling terrorism voluntarily

Acknowledgement

As this is a new approach that we have followed of searching for links in research-findings that when strung together, would give an overall picture of what exactly life is, and the various phenomena linked with it, such as creation, birth, death, cosmic laws that govern life on earth, of changes with the passage of time, of the phenomenon of evolution, there were very few people who had thought on these lines, though many suggested very helpful literature. So we have had to rely on literature, and our own discussions as to what research findings to include, and in what order, so as to present the picture of a changing world with the growing consciousness and knowledge in every field that would enlighten us about the Truth regarding the process of creation, of growth and evolution, of death and reincarnation, and the overall objective of life. This is the result of a combined research of two authors - a research scientist and a social activist who would understand the significance of research findings in the improvement of society and social behavior.

Prema Edwina Bedell and Theo Vaes

INTRODUCTION

THIS book is all about the unraveling of some of the misunderstood phenomena of the world we live in, at first by the great Greek Thinkers of the ancient world, followed by the painstaking experiments, analyses, and interpretations of the European Scientists of the eighteenth century onwards. The early beliefs were that the earth was flat and fixed in space and the sun and other planets revolved round the earth. People all over the world were under the impression that all things are as God made them and nothing can change. Anyone who differed from this idea was blaspheming and challenging God's authority. But as experiments of science progressed, it found explanations for the phenomena hitherto firmly rooted in the human mind (as best taken on faith and left unquestioned) began to change.

Even today, evolution still remains a controversial and a much misunderstood subject, mostly because people seem to be talking at cross purposes, and not concentrating on getting the definitions right. If we define evolution as changes that take place with the passage of time, it would be easy to observe the changes, and find a scientific explanation for them. That is what we have presented in this book. Another term which seems to be misunderstood is the term 'life' which even the most learned scientists seem to be confusing with 'life-forms'. This is a term coined by us to denote all creations. Here again is a word that is linked in the minds of people with religion, because they have not thought of the mechanism of creation. We have regarded creation as a union of energy with matter. Regarding the term 'life' we feel it has to be abstract and should not be something that can be created or destroyed in a laboratory. But for a proper understanding of what is meant by abstract, we have to visualize this abstract thing called 'life'. The only abstract thing that we could think of, that cannot be created or destroyed is energy; but energy cannot be separated from time and space, because energy occupies space, and when it expresses itself, it has to do so in a given space, at a particular point of time. So we concluded that life is made up of space energy and time. This is of course speculation. But it helps us to visualize many phenomena which may be proved by scientific observations and analyses.

We have traced the findings of some ancient Greek Thinkers, followed by those of the more modern European scientists mainly on the changing nature of things, in spite of which they can still be grouped and classified such as: (1) The changes in the terrain brought about by earthquakes, eruption of volcanoes, land erosions, disappearance of rivers underground, up lift of mountains, etc. (2) Changes in the distribution of land masses brought about by the continental drift (3) Changing nature of flora and fauna in different geological periods as evident by fossil records and brought about by periodic changes in the global climate (4)The existence of law and order in all forms of creations enabling them to be classified and grouped (i.e. Appendix 2A and 2B) (5) And how scientists have come to the conclusion that the earliest life-forms were unicellular beings and have progressed from thereon to multicellular and more complex forms. It is here that our ideas get confused, because so far, we have concentrated only on Human Beings and how this group has the complex form it does. We have not thought about how the multi cellular mass has got differentiated into different distinct groups of plants and animals, which can be arranged in groups of increasing complexity. As no one seems to have taken up this study, we have mistaken the role of chromosomes and genes in bringing about changes as exclusive, and have considered the resemblance of humans to monkeys, and taken humans to be mutated monkeys. Yet no thought has been given to the fact that some humans do resemble other animals like horses, rabbits, camels, giraffes, ants, bats, lions etc in their facial structure and expression, teeth, and body language. Yet no one has thought of them as mutations from these animals.

We have given an explanation for the changes in form being brought about by an increase in consciousness of the energy that pervades the whole multi cellular mass, combined with the inherent traits within that unit of energy, when it first united with matter to create a life-form. The idea of inherent traits is based on the fact that life contains both good and evil in latent form. The new point we have brought out here is that there are two lines of control in every life-form and those are (1) one controlled by inherent traits present in the energy that pervades the whole of the individual's body which gives it a given form with particular abstract traits. (2) The other line of control is the chromosomes and genes that are responsible for the maintenance of the physical structure and shapes of the organisms.

Everything in life, as well as every step of life is governed by cosmic laws. In order to understand these laws, it is necessary to have knowledge of different subjects, such as physics, nuclear physics, chemistry, biology, biochemistry, biophysics, mathematics, geology, genetics, microbiology, oceanography, paleontology, evolution, cell biology, astronomy, as well as different branches of social sciences. All these have been brought out in this book in an elementary form. So this book can be classified as an Introductory Text Book of General Science for students passing out of school. This will enable them to find the link between the different subjects they have to study, and achievement of the objective of life; so that they can try to make this a safer and more progressive world to come back to from time to time in different reincarnations. They will also understand why they should strive to remove all their negative traits by practicing self control, instead of trying to remove the stress they are under, by temporary relief with alcohol, drugs, sex, and various rituals. Further, they will come to know what is meant by, 'life has both good and evil, and though evil has power, it is invariably overcome by the good'; because good is the manifested positive force, and evil is the manifested negative force, and life is a neutral force which contains both good and evil in latent forms. When we speak of life having both good and evil, what we mean is good emotions and evil emotions. We have always to keep in mind that emotions are the driving power in all Beings. This book is also useful for laymen in understanding the Law of Karma that controls the destiny of all living Beings.Also, if the law of karma (which states that every action has a reaction equal and opposite) is kept in mind, intelligent people will be wary of their thoughts, words, and actions, and will avoid violence, injustice and terrorism. Seeking out the truths is not just an academic exercise. It has practical implications and is meant to become a part of every individual's life to achieve peace and harmony, and freedom from guilt and fear, and thus bring about an overall improvement in society.

HIDDEN TRUTHS

I GNORANCE is like the sphinx, which has the face and voice of a virgin, wings of a bird, and claws of a griffin, who poses difficult riddles to those who attempt to cross the boundaries of her realm. Unless these riddles are solved, they torment and worry the mind, pulling it first this way and then that way, tearing it apart. The great eternal truths and the principles of life existed long before humans appeared on earth. When each individual unit of life went through several reincarnations, and finally evolved into a human, from a long line of life- forms, growing at first in consciousness, awareness, and knowledge, and later in wisdom, and sensitivity in small degrees through several more incarnations as humans, it took several centuries to reach their present level of evolution. They now began getting curious about the life around them, and wondered where they came from, and where their ultimate destination was. So began the search for their roots.

In the dim past, the world that existed was very different from what it is today. There were no humans, no houses, no roads, no shops, no vehicles, no cultivation and no trade. There were only rocks and soil and perhaps the beginnings of some very primitive life- forms, so tiny that they were hardly visible, to the naked eye.

Man in his evolved state, has had to apply the knowledge he had gained through the centuries, in various fields of his endeavors, and piece together evidences bit by bit, before he even began to get an idea of the different life-forms on this earth, and man's relationship to other life-forms. Further, he also found that life-forms, that existed in the beginning, and which populated the earth then, were very different from the life-forms of today. The search is still on, because evidences of truths are scattered here and there.

As time went on, life-forms gradually evolved from tiny one celled Beings like bacteria, virus, amoeba etc, when one unit of energy combined with one unit of matter. Each life-form so created had to compete with each other, for space as well as interact with each other. It also had to multiply itself, because with the awakening of consciousness, comes a diluted form of awareness of space, time, and self. The first life-forms however seem to be the elements such as hydrogen, helium, nitrogen, carbon, phosphorus etc of which there are a total of 92 elements. These were formed from energy itself which then joined together to form shapeless masses called nebulae, which subsequently got differentiated into galaxies containing millions of stars, suns, planets, moons, satellites, and asteroids all of which spun on their own axis for fixed periods of time, indicating an awareness of time, and orbited around a chosen sun in a fixed path indicating an awareness of space. These millions of stars also grouped themselves into different shaped galaxies of different sizes and colors. The generally accepted theory of the birth of the universe however is the Big Bang Theory, according to which an enormously large object burst with a bang and the pieces scattered into space and produced all the heavenly bodies. But this does not explain how each of these heavenly bodies spun on their own axis and completed a whole circle in a fixed period of time, nor does it explain how each of them came to be global in shape, and got differentiated into stars, suns, planets, and satellites.

Each planet spins round its own axis and completes a full circle in a fixed period of time indicating an awareness of time. Further, it orbits round the sun in a fixed path, indicating an awareness of space. These stars, planets etc are not generally counted among life-forms, and yet they are believed to have a life period. Also they are made up of compressed elements which themselves are a part of energy. So it is presumed that they can be taken as life-forms of a primitive type which are at the early stages of developing consciousness. The stars, planets etc seem to have a fixed life period, after which they seem to be gobbled up by the black hole. During their life period, which extends to billions of years, they seem to go through various stages of development such as formation of land masses and water bodies, development of atmospheres, and union of units of energy with units of matter called plasma, to form primitive unicellular life-forms. In the beginning, these life-forms were also conscious of only space, time, and self, and competed with each other for space. Later developments were the desire for self preservation, and self multiplication. Then perhaps the tiny blobs of plasma each energized by a unit of energy began to grow by union with other similar blobs of plasma, and in the next reincarnation developed a tiny gene, and a cell membrane which helped each of the blobs of plasma to keep its own individual identity. It may be noted that the gene as well as the cell membrane are made up of proteins which are the building blocks of all life-forms.

As time moved on, these unicellular life-forms gained more and more consciousness and awareness, and with it came the desire for self expression. This was accompanied by awareness of the advantage of self multiplication and living in groups, and still later, the necessity for division of labor. It may be noted that from the time prokaryotic cells got reincarnated into eukaryotic cells, there was a differentiation of the eukaryotic cells that were to develop into members of the plant kingdom and those that were to develop into the members of the animal kingdom.(Appendix 4). The next step was to demarcate the whole mass of cells to form three parts. In the plant kingdom, the three parts formed the crown, stem, and roots; and in the animal kingdom, they formed the head, trunk and limbs. The mystery here is how the multi cellular mass of cells divided itself into the three portions to form the crown stem and roots of the plant kingdom, or head trunk and limbs of the animal kingdom, and took on the form of different members of the plant and animal kingdoms. Another mystery is how each cell of the multi cellular mass became aware of the distinct identity of its own group, so as to know whether it belonged to groups that were to form the head, the trunk, or the limbs, or as in the plant kingdom, the groups that were to form the crown, stem, or roots. Further, we have to presume that the different life-forms such as ants, insects, birds or rabbits as examples, developed into their respective forms depending on their inherent characteristics.

Studies carried out in the last few decades indicate that the cells of the different parts of the body vary not only in shape, but also in the structure of the protein molecules that form the building blocks of the different organs. Further, that each cell is a highly organized manufacturing unit, which not only manufactures the requirements of the organs it is responsible for, but also reproduces itself, so that the manufacturing process is not interrupted when it dies. So, from a unicellular life-form, that had only consciousness of space, time, and self, it has reincarnated into a multi cellular life-form differentiated into organs composed of highly organized cells, each part of which, knows its own role in the process of growth. The next question that comes up while pondering about the development of consciousness and awareness and their consequences, is whether the directing and guiding hand behind it all, is an outside force, or is the force located in the body itself. As energy which is a part of life itself, is permeated through the entire body, it is this energy which is gaining more and more consciousness and awareness and a primitive type of knowledge with the passage of time. So it may be presumed that these changes are the result of the increase in consciousness of the energy that is pervading the whole life-form, and the changes are taking place from within. In fact, each individual life-form has its own identity through its DNA which is part of its own chromosome structure, and which has developed through the individual cell's knowledge of its own potentials. Chromosomes are the limiting factors which are the embodiment of the law, that like begets like. So each group of life-forms has its own chromosome number, and chromosome structure, which keeps it within certain limits of size and form. It is only when some mutations happen within the chromosomes, during mitosis and meiosis, or during some extreme environmental conditions, that changes can take place in the life-form and that also, would be within the limits of which the life-form belongs.

However, great changes in life-forms have been taking place from time to time, following phenomenal changes in the environment due to climatic changes, and rearrangement of land masses for which chromosomes and genes cannot be held responsible. As time moved on, some life-forms have become extinct, and newer and newer life-forms have come into existence, new forms of vegetation, new forms of insect and animal life, and finally came the appearance of man. The general observation so far is, that a unit of life once created cannot be annihilated and that no life-form comes ready- made. It may therefore be presumed that the units of energy which were part of the extinct life-forms, have now taken on new forms such as the human form for better ways and more organized ways of life and adjustment to the environment.. Also once a unit of energy has combined with a unit of matter to create a life-form, it can only change forms, but cannot be annihilated, nor can it rejoin the original life stream which consists of a neutral force, with latent positive force, and latent negative force. So it may be presumed that among the extinct life-forms, those that had developed a higher level of consciousness and awareness became humans.

The humans that existed in those days were very different from the humans as they are now. They were more animal-like, as they spoke no language, and did not know how to communicate with each other, they ate raw flesh, and wore no clothes, and lived singly in caves. Their only activities were to hunt for food, fight each other for space and mates and reproduce. This is evidence enough to conclude that humans did not come ready-made in the human form; but have evolved from animal forms through reincarnations which may not necessarily be an ape, as is the general belief. The belief that humans have evolved from the mutation of an ape has some serious flaws. Firstly, for this to be true, many apes all over the world would have to mutate at the same time in a similar way, which does not really seem possible. It may be that different humans have had different paths of evolution because, many times we see individuals that resemble horses, dogs, cats, rabbits, snakes, fishes, elephants, lions, monkeys, bats, ants, and even pigs in some of their facial features and expressions, teeth, and even body language. So the change in form has to come from the consciousness within the evolving life-form, depending on the inherent qualities present in the unit of energy, when it first combined with the unit of matter. This may also be an explanation for the great variations, one finds in human nature all over the world, irrespective of race, religion, country and social norms.

The beginning of man's march into civilization may be attributed to his first yearnings for self expression, when he began to make pictures on the walls of caves, and on bones, and horns of animals. In order to do this, he had to make tools out of stones. While he was making tools, rubbing one stone against another, he may have accidentally set a whole forest on fire, roasting animals which could not escape. And when he ate the roasted animals, he started cooking, and living in groups along riversides.

From the time humans began living in groups and began sharing their talents, knowledge and skills, they found it necessary to express themselves in speech. So they began by standardizing different sounds for different objects. This was the beginning of the development of communication skills. This was followed by learning to count, weigh, and measure, write, and record, and so began the first steps of trading. When such activities led to disputes, they found the need to have a leader, and so began the idea of having kings and kingdoms. A study of history shows, that around 10000 BC, several riverside civilizations had sprung up such as Sumerian, Egyptian, Persian, Greek, Indian, and Chinese.

Humanity had now come a long way from an animal-like existence, and had knowledge of agriculture, manufacturing of domestic articles, building of dwelling places, manufacturing of weapons for self defense, and had expanded their trade to far off places, and had domesticated animals to help them in their daily activities. As their knowledge increased, with the passage of time, they also became aware of the inevitability of birth and death. An idea struck them that there are two forces, one which was good and benevolent, and gave them life and light and freedom from fear of the unknown. The other which was dark and mysterious and filled them with the fear of the unknown, especially death. They regarded death as the work of evil forces that dwelt deep down in the earth, where they buried their dead, and from where the bodies disappeared. It was dark deep down in the earth and they were ignorant as to what happened to the dead. As they identified themselves wholly with their bodies, they had no knowledge of the soul, or a life after death. So they felt that the evil force that existed deep down in the recesses of the earth, came out when they were hungry, and killed and ate the humans and that was the end of them.

So the early humans felt that it was necessary to propitiate the benevolent forces, such as the sun, fire, rain, thunder etc which protected them from evil forces, and also helped them to grow their food by supplying them with rain. The thunder they thought was the war cry which kept the evil forces at bay. The sun they regarded as their chief protector, and they felt that it travelled round the earth everyday specially to protect the humans from the evil forces. After a long period of time when awareness developed into knowledge, man began looking for reasons beyond the whims of the gods as the ultimate answer as to why the world they lived in, was the way it was. Archeological findings have shown, that by this time, the ancient Sumerians and Egyptians had more than a rudimentary knowledge of medicine, astronomy, applied mathematics, and engineering. But even much later, importance was given by different civilizations, to different phenomenon. Thales of Miletus thought that the prime substance on earth was water, Anaxagoras believed it to be air, and Xenophanes proposed that mud was the main substance. The ancient Hindus believed fire to be the main substance as it was a purifying factor.

It was however, the Greek Thinkers who first began looking for underlying principles which could form the basis of more satisfactory answers, where one phenomenon could be linked to the other. This was the beginning of man's rejection of trust in 'truth by authority'. So began the search for causes and principles based on observation and reasoning. Then Truth became the province of the Thinkers rather than the Priests. The Thinkers were responsible for the development of the subject called science. The aim of science is to describe and explain the world we live in, and man's every step can be considered as a quest for reality, which is the hidden truths.

The physical laws that govern two fundamental forces of the universe namely, gravitation and electromagnetism produce nearly all the phenomena of nature. Electricity and magnetism were in the beginning regarded as two separate entities. It was the experiments of Oersted and Faraday in the 19th century AD which demonstrated that a current of electricity is always surrounded by a magnetic field, and that under certain conditions, magnetic forces can induce electrical currents. Thus electricity and magnetism came to be considered as a single force known as the electromagnetic force which controls all other forces of nature, such as (1) chemical forces which hold atoms together in molecules, (2) the cohesive force which bind together the larger particles of matter, (3) elastic force which help bodies to maintain their shapes even during growth (4) frictional forces which is an interplay of matter, as all matter are composed of atoms which in turn are composed of electrical particles. Science however cannot really explain what electricity is, or what magnetism is, or what gravitation is, although their effects can be measured and predicted. But of their ultimate nature, even modern scientists are quite blank. These are some of the hidden Truths of life and so are space, energy, and time, which are present everywhere all at the same time, and are part of all life activities, and cannot be created or destroyed, or described. They are a trinity and have to work together as a whole, because energy occupies space and when energy expresses itself, it has to do so in a particular space, at a particular point of time. So it may be presumed that the three are inseparable like three parts of one body.

There are also other hidden Truths for which satisfactory answers are still to be found as they are still under speculation; such as (1) the progress of life-forms from unicellular to multi cellular mass of cells which then gets differentiated into different groups of plant and animal life-forms;; (2) the development of each cell of a complex organism into a highly organized cell system; (3) the first appearance of chromosomes and genes; (4) and how they are made to control the size, shape, and form, as well as maintain the longevity of groups of life-forms; (5)and how DNA of the chromosomes maintains the identity of the individual; (6) The process of evolution too is still partly a mystery, especially macro evolution which involves reincarnation and a complete change of form such as when different types of vegetation and different types of animals came into being.(7) Another mystery is how within a lifetime, the form changes with the process of growth, without the chromosomes and genes being involved and the precision with which they take place in a whole group with the passage of time at regular intervals. But these problems have to be tackled first by speculation and then by experimentation just as the ancients have done, and have come so far in the search for the roots of the humans.

SCATTERED EVIDENCES
OF TRUTH

T HE great thinkers of the ancient world were Greeks. It was an intellectual pastime for them to search for general abstract Truths. During the process, what they discovered made their work more important than what they themselves realized, because the methods they developed could be used for many similar situations. For instance, Thales of Miletus stunned the Egyptians when he showed them how the methods used for measuring the height of triangles could be used for measuring the height of pyramids, as well as the distance of a ship at sea.

Euclid was another Greek who in 300 BC showed that the different phenomena on this earth could be understood only by the application of reason, rather than by revealed knowledge. He wrote and published a book called 'The Elements' which has stood the test of time. It is the most widely translated and prescribed book for the study of mathematics even in modern times. His work is important because it led to a whole new way of thinking in which, the way to Truth can be found by logic, deductive reasoning, evidence and proof, rather than by intuition and faith. Euclid's great achievement was to combine the knowledge of geometry of his day into a coherent framework of basic theory and proofs which is the basis of all aspects of science even today. Among Euclid's key postulates are two, which according to us are of great importance in visualizing infinity, and these are (1) part of a line can be drawn between two given points, and (2) such a part line can be extended indefinitely on both sides.

Another method of visualizing infinity is by the concept of the zero in the Hindu numbering system, brought to the western world by an Arab called Al-Khwarzmi in 500 AD. In the Hindu numeral system described by Al-Khwarzmi, the numerals start from 0 and go on from one to nine and from then on, the zeros are put after each digit in turn, so that 1 becomes 10 and 10 becomes100, 1000, 10000, 100000, 1000000 and so on to infinity with the addition of zeros. So that zero becomes an infinite continuity factor, because a repetition of zeros makes space for expansion of a number indefinitely and can go on to infinity. Still another system introduced by Al-Khwarzmi himself was Algebra, which by using symbols for numbers can go on to infinity.

Aristotle was a Greek Philosopher whose ideas on natural science dominated the western world for two thousand years. He believed that for man to understand the ultimate truth, he must begin by reasoning from self evident principles, such as things that fall to the ground belong to the earth, and things that rise up belong to the sky. He aimed at finding out why things happen as they do, and not how things happen as they do.

Actually modern science came into being when Galileo began to reason out how things happen and this was the beginning of experimental science. Galileo's discoveries were followed by Newton in the next century, and thus were born the ideas of a universe governed by forces, pressures, waves, oscillations, and tensions. But with the passage of time, Newton's laws of mechanics which seemed at the time so accurate began exhibiting deviations of a very fundamental nature in the invisible realm of atoms, and in the fathomless depths of intergalactic space. Between the years 1900 AD and 1927 AD two theoretical systems were developed to explain the above mentioned phenomena of atoms and of intergalactic space namely (1) the quantum theory dealing with fundamental units of matter and energy and (2) the theory of relativity dealing mainly with space and time, and in a general way the structure of the universe.

But before the world came to this stage of knowledge, it had to undergo many twists and turns such as for instance, in the 15th century AD the world believed that the earth was still, and fixed, at the centrè of the universe, and around the earth the sun, moon, planets, and stars, revolved in perfect circles. In 1490 AD when Nicolas Copernicus a Priest and Astronomer from Europe was in his twenties, he suggested that it was the sun which was at the centre, and not the earth, and all the planets revolved around sun. In 1514 AD Copernicus published a hand written book for his friends in which he suggested that the time taken for each planet to complete its cycle increases, the further it is from the sun. For example Mercury which is closest to the sun takes 88 days, Venus takes 225 days, Earth takes 365 days that is one year, Mars takes one year and nine months, Jupiter takes 12 years, and Saturn takes 30 years to complete one cycle.

It is Galileo Galilee who is recognized as the father of science, and was a brilliant Thinker and Inventor of the 16th century AD that first invented a telescope and studied the night sky. He made many observations such as (a) that there were many mountains and valleys on the moon, and (b) Venus has phases like the moon, (c) and the sun has sun spots. It was some of these observations that convinced Galileo that Copernicus was right when he suggested that the sun was the centre of the universe and not the earth. Galileo insisted on the importance of experimentation, observations, and demonstrations. His greatest achievements were in understanding how things move. This created the basis for the modern science of physics. Earlier for nearly 2000 years the world unquestioningly accepted Aristotle's views, but Galileo with his observations paved the way for Newton's views on gravity, motion, and force. He did some experiments to show the error of Aristotle's views that heavier things fall down faster. This he did by dropping cannon balls of different sizes and different weights from the Leaning Tower of Pisa. He showed beyond doubt that they land at the same time. These ideas later developed into the science of Mechanics by combining Physics and Mathematics.

Galileo was also interested in mathematics and was impressed with the works of ancient Greeks like Archimedes who was born in 287 BC in Sicily, which was then a Greek colony. Archimedes tried to approach every problem mathematically even small ones like if two weights are put on a seesaw, the lighter one must be closer to the centre than the heavier one to balance it. He showed that the ratio of weights to one another goes down in exact mathematical proportion to the distance from the pivot of the seesaw. Another of Archimedes insight was that every object on earth has a centre of gravity which is a single point of balance from which all its weight seems to hang. Besides putting practical phenomena mathematically, Archimedes also used mathematical principals to solve practical problems. He showed that the surface area of a sphere is four times the area of a circle with the same radius. Further he also showed that the volume of a sphere is two thirds of a cylinder into which it fits perfectly. However he is best known for his invention of pulleys and levers used to launch giant ships.

Hipparchus was another ancient Greek who was a great astronomer considering that he had no telescopes and had to use his own naked eyes, and some vague historical records to guide him. He depended mainly on his mathematical skill. It is believed that Hipparchus was the inventor of the branch of mathematics known as trigonometry (the mathematics of triangles.). He developed the first trigonometric tables which helped him calculate the precise position of a star in the sky relative to the earth and other stars. One of the most important calculations made by Hipparchus came about when he plotted the ecliptic which is the circular path of the sun through the sky. The ecliptic is at an angle to the earth's equator, and crosses the equator at two points known as equinoxes, and one which takes the sun farthest away from it at the solstices. Hipparchus then noticed that though the sun apparently travelled a circular path, the time taken for the solstices and equinoxes were not of equal length. In order to get an explanation for this, he worked out a method of calculating the sun's path which would show its exact location in any given day. Further, he also measured the length of a year as precisely as possible by measuring the time between equinoxes and comparing it with ancient records. He arrived at a figure which was just 6 minutes off the mark. Hipparchus then went on to calculate the exact timing and position of the stars at the equinoxes, and compared it with observations taken 150 years earlier. He observed that the stars near the ecliptic had moved their position slightly and came to the conclusion that the whole star pattern was moving slowly eastwards, and that it would go round and return to the same position every 26000 years. It is now known that this change is brought about by a slow change in the direction of the earth's tilt and is known as precession. So the calculation made by Hipparchus was basically correct, though his conclusion about the movement of the star pattern was off the mark.

In spite of the findings of the ancient observers, it took the world several centuries to realize that the world was very old, and it was a changing world, where the geography and terrain were changing at intervals. The general idea up to the 18th century AD was that the only change that took place was during the great deluge mentioned in the Bible. It was James Hutton who first suggested in 1785 AD, that it was the earth's internal heat and pressure that was responsible for molten rocks to emerge as volcanoes, and that the earth's geography were not made once and for all. Slow continuous changes were taking place with countless erosions, sedimentations, and uplift of hills and mountains, that repeated over long periods of time.

Due to the ideas introduced by Galileo and later Newton, the world now knew something about why things moved and what things are made of. However as chemistry was still in its infancy, people still believed that there were only four elements and those are air, water, earth, and fire.

Alfred Lothar Wagener was the first one to suggest that landmasses broke up and drifted apart at intervals (Appendix 3). He was the youngest child of Dr Richard Wegener an evangelical minister in Berlin. Alfred Wegener was trained in astronomy and got his doctorate in 1904 AD. But he took up a profession in meteorology when he was invited to join an expedition to study polar air flows in the unmapped eastern coast of Greenland. Alfred Lothar Wagener suggested that the division of land and sea was not fixed once and for all. He believed that the hottest deserts had once been under the Polar ice caps and that moving continents were part of a mechanism that included other activities of the earth such as earthquakes, erupting volcanoes, movement of magnetic poles, and up thrust of hills and mountains. But he could not convince the professional geologists who dismissed him as an amateur, propounding dangerous ideas. In 1911 AD Alfred Wegener came across a research paper in the university library that listed fossils of plants and animals on both sides of the Atlantic Ocean. The scientists explained the similarities by suggesting that land bridges had once spanned the ocean, but they had sunk without leaving a trace when the earth contracted. But Alfred Wegener was not convinced. He felt that there was in the beginning one big land mass that split up and drifted apart (Appendix 3). Wegener believed that the continents were not deep rooted in the earth. They were actually floating over the rocky surface under the ocean. But he had no convincing explanation to show how land masses moved around in the ocean. There was however a few scientists who supported Wegener, such as Alfred Holmes a professor at Edinburgh University who suggested that convection currents deep within the earth might move the continents. But Wegener realized that he would have to produce some convincing supporting evidence for his theories. So He studied geological features as well as fossil records, on both sides of the Atlantic Ocean. He mapped bands of mountains and deposits of coal and minerals, and it showed continuous strips, running from Africa to South America. However, it was when he made a study of paleo-climatology (that is, the climate patterns millions of years ago) with the help of Vladimir Koppen, and plotted ancient jungles, and deserts, and ice sheets, on the original land mass, that supporting evidence to his theories started adding up. This period Wagener was working on, was known as the permo carboniferous ice age which occurred 280 million years ago.(Appendix 1)

It was twenty years after Wegener's death in 1950 AD, that new scientific methods were developed in oceanography (that is, examination of the seafloor) and paleo-magnetism (that is, studies on how magnetic polarity of the earth has shifted over millions of years) that evidence in support of Wegener's theory of moving land masses became established. There is now the Plate Tectonics Theory which explains the movement of the land masses suggested by Wagener. According to this theory the landmasses are divided into a top level mantle, and below is a thick sticky liquid rock at a very high temperature known as magna. The mantle which is divided into a number of large and small plates float on top of the magna, and their movement is as described by Wagener as the continental drift. However, Wagener was incorrect in thinking that only the land plates moved. He did not know about the magna on which the plates rested. It is now possible to trace the movement of these plates over millions of years.

During the end of the 18th century AD both scientists and some theologians began wondering about the mechanism of creations, especially when scientists collected large amounts of specimens of life-forms, and noted that each was perfectly suited to its environment as well as its way of life. For example fishes had structures which enabled them to swim and live in water; insects and birds had wings to fly and lived on trees; while purely terrestrial Beings had limbs to walk and work with, and found or made themselves dwelling places to live in. There were also animals called amphibians that lived partly in water and partly on land; these had skin and body structures that could swim in water and leap around on terrestrial ground, for example frogs. Scientists also found that all creatures without exception, both animals and plants could be classified and grouped in an orderly manner, starting from a broad class of more or less similar general characteristics, to smaller and smaller groups of more specific characteristics. The individuals of the lower group called species could interbreed.(Appendix 2A and 2B)

The general belief in those days was that everything that existed was created by God who shaped them with invisible hands, and they remained unchanged. But soon some Naturalists began looking at fossil vegetation and animal remains and found them very different from the existing ones. Soon people began getting conscious of the fact that not only vegetation and animals, but even the terrain of the lands were changing due to cycles of erosion and upheavals. One of the great Thinkers of those times was Erasmus Darwin – grandfather of Charles Darwin, who argued that life-forms were definitely changing with time. Another great Thinker of those times, was the French Naturalist Lamarck, who visualized that life-forms changed in a purposeful manner, from one celled organisms to the complex structure of humans, because each had an 'inner feeling' which propelled it into developing more and more complex structures. He also argued that skills which helped it to survive could be passed on to the next generation and build up from one generation to the other. The world society in those days were way behind Lamarck's thinking and so could not accept his ideas and even vilified him and his supporters.

It was much later that Charles Darwin came into the picture. He was born in February 1809 AD and his father was a doctor, who wanted his son also to be a doctor. But Charles met a zoologist called Robert Grant a great believer in Lamarck's views. A little later he was also distracted by another Naturalist called Reverend Professor John Henslowe, with whom he formed a firm bond, and the two of them would often go specimen hunting. In 1830 AD Henslowe was invited to join a trip to South America on a surveying trip. As Henslowe could not go, he suggested that Charles Darwin go instead of him. This voyage which was initially meant for two years lasted five years. During this time Darwin gathered a large number of specimens from around the world, and learnt enough about wild life at close range. Darwin concentrated on working out what exactly evolution was meant to be. He concentrated on individuals, rather than the species, and showed that individuals evolve by natural selection and that within a group there are variations indicating that some individuals are better equipped to survive under a given environment, than others. Thus was born the saying 'survival of the fittest'.

Darwin continued working on his ideas of evolution and

published a book called "Origin of the Species". There were both praises and condemnation on the ideas presented in the book. Some at once accepted the ideas because they seemed to be a plausible explanation for the variations encountered in nature even within a species. Others condemned the idea, because they did not like to think of humans who they believed was made in the image of God, being descended from a monkey. This misunderstanding came about, we believe, because they thought humans were mutations of monkeys. They failed to link it with Lamarck's idea that life-forms evolve into a higher and more complex forms due to an 'inner feeling'. In fact the idea that humans are mutations from monkeys have some serious points against it. First of all, for such a thing to happen, many monkeys all over the world have to mutate at the same time, which is most unlikely. Then again all the different life-forms that have come up originally from single cell organisms and developed into complex organisms with head, trunk, and limbs were not thought to be mutations. So these changes had to come from within, as visualized by Lamarck. This is where the process of reincarnation in macro evolution offers a plausible explanation, especially when we consider that the changes are taking place in an individual in subsequent life times, and not within any given lifetime. Thinking along these lines calls for some mental acrobatics, because when we speak of lifetimes we are referring to an individual's reincarnations. But when we speak of generations we are referring to parent progeny situations.

A great contributor to the understanding of the truths of life, specifically about the nature of inheritance is Gregor Mendel -a monk in the Augustinian monastery of Brun in Moravia (modern day Czech Republic). He was the first person to use mathematics and applied statistics in biology. He is now recognized as having laid the foundation to the modern science of genetics. Mendel's interest in plants started from the time when he worked on his father's orchard and farm.

Mendel started his experiments on seven varieties of peas initially to observe if they bred true. Each one was bred for a given trait such as tallness or shortness, differences in pod size and shape, differences in color and position of flowers on the stem, and color and nature of seed coat. After observing that they bred true, he repeatedly cross bred these varieties. He grew 30000 plants for his experiments in a period of seven years. He noted down even small variations, and the exact number of each trait observed. This helped him to make statistical analyses, and observe patterns of variations and ratios of each trait.

The results of Mendel's experiments were that the first generation of cross bred plants (known technically as F1 hybrids) showed the traits of only one parent. For instance yellow seeded plants when crossed with green seeded plants produced all plants with yellow seeds; and tall stemmed plants when crossed with short stemmed plants produced all tall stemmed plants. This indicated that the trait of one parent was dominant and showed up. Now the question arose as to what happened to the trait of the other parent, that is the green seeded plants. Mendel came to the conclusion that the trait which did not show up was still there, but it was recessive. The second result was when Mendel crossed the plants of the F1 generation he found the recessive trait now reappeared in constant proportions in each experiment that is, in F2 generation three quarters of the plants showed the dominant trait, and one quarter showed the recessive trait. From this, Mendel concluded that each parent plant carries a pair of traits such as yellow and green seeds, tall and short stems etc. These pairs were later termed as genes. Mendel realized that each parent plant carries a pair of genes for each trait which passed on to their offspring during reproduction, and that out of the pair, one can be dominant. Also these genes do not blend or form a mixture with each other. He further concluded that when the hybrid plant developed, then in the reproductive cells (technically known as gametes) the genes segregate and pass to different gametes. The offspring (technically known as progeny) inherits from a parent either one trait or the other, but never both together. This is known as Mendel's first law, that is, the principle of segregation. By applying this law in several succeeding generations, Mendel was able to predict accurately the number of progeny exhibiting each trait.

Mendel tried another experiment by crossing pea plants that differed in two or more traits. He found that these traits reappeared in different combinations in the progenies, that is, wrinkled seeds with fat pods, smooth seeds with thin pods etc. But segregation of pod shape occurred independently of the segregation of seed surface, and traits combined with each other at random. This pertains to Mendel's second law, that is, the principle of independent assortment.

When Mendel published his findings, scientists were not ready to recognize it as a ground breaking work, leading to a new approach. It was only after his death that his work's importance came to light, and it was recognized to have general application to all organisms including humans. Scientists now continue to use the statistical methods pioneered by Mendel to explore the complex world of genetic transmission, which in turn has led to an understanding of genetics at a molecular level leading to the discovery of DNA and RNA molecules (Appendix 5). Such an understanding of Genetics has revolutionized modern life not only in breeding experiments and improving and tailoring crops, and in the field of medicine to eliminate inherited diseases, but also in solving crimes.

In 1895 AD Wilhelm Rontgen a German Physicist discovered some electromagnetic rays that came to be known as X-rays. In 1896 AD the French Physicist Antoine Henri Becquerel reported that uranium salt produced similar rays. But it was subsequently named Becquerel rays. The discovery of these rays started the nuclear age and opened up a whole new field of research. Marie Curie a French scientist of Polish origin and a student of Becquerel began researching on which elements gave off similar emissions. In 1898 Marie Curie coined the term 'radioactive' to describe the elements that gave off the mystery rays. During her work she found that the compound pitchblende produced more radioactivity than uranium. The processing of pitchblende was tedious. It had to be ground down a kilo at a time, and sieved before being boiled, and continually stirred for hours to form a liquid which could be distilled. Finally when the liquid was electrolyzed a minute amount of radioactive element was isolated. Soon Pierre, her husband joined her in the Project and together in 1898 they discovered polonium. But soon the couple discovered that the pitchblende contained yet another element which was even more radioactive. In 1903 the Curies as well as Becquerel were given the Nobel Prize for Physics for their work on radioactive elements. Radioactivity was Marie's life work. In 1911 she was awarded the Nobel Prize for chemistry, for her work on polonium and radium.

However, it was Ernest Rutherford of New Zealand who did more than anyone else to reveal the true nature of radioactivity and to explain the architecture of the atom so much so, that he may be considered to have laid the foundation for the new discipline of nuclear physics. In 1895 AD Rutherford left New Zealand to work with Professor Thomson at the University of Cambridge. Here he invented a mechanism that could detect electromagnetic waves over a distance of a few meters and even pass through walls. In 1896 Professor Thomson asked Rutherford to help him investigate the effects of passing X-rays through a gas. They discovered that X-rays when passed through gas produced great quantities of ions (that is, atoms that have acquired either a positive or negative electric charge by losing one or more electrons) and that these ions then recombine to form neutral molecules. Later Rutherford by himself worked out a method to measure the speed at which ions recombine. He also worked on the nature of radioactivity and found that when radioactivity is passed through air, it produces two distinct types of rays. The first type he named them alpha rays. They produced very large quantities of ions which were easily absorbed by a surface. He named the second type as beta rays. These produced fewer ions which penetrated much deeper than the surface. He found that these rays could pass through an aluminum foil one fifth of millimeter thick. In 1898 Rutherford teamed up with a young chemist called Fredrick Soddy and studied the phenomenon of radioactivity in three elements that is Thorium, Radium, and Actinium. They noticed that thorium disintegrated into gas, which in turn disintegrated into an unknown new element which was extremely radioactive, and the radioactivity eventually made the new element disappear. Rutherford and Soddy then concluded that radioactivity was a process by which atoms of one element spontaneously changed into atoms of a different element which was also radioactive. But scientists were diffident to accept this finding because it seemed like medieval alchemy. In 1908 further experimentation proved the correctness of Rutherford's and Soddy's conclusion. During their experiments with radioactive elements, they observed that these substances decayed half quantities at a time at a fixed rate, and the other portion which decayed subsequently also took the same time. This they saw while working with thorium. One half decayed in four days and the other half also decayed in four days subsequently. Rutherford immediately saw the practical implication to this phenomenon. He realized that the half life and steady rate of decay could be used to measure the age of a piece of rock by measuring the amount of radiation it contained. This was the beginning of a new branch of science known as radiometric dating. Another discovery made by Rutherford was when he passed alpha rays through a thin glass wall of a container connected to an outer glass tube and found that the collected gas was helium, thus concluding that alpha rays were in fact ionized helium atoms stripped of their electrons.

By the end of the nineteenth century AD the mysteries surrounding gravity, motion, electromagnetism, gas, optics etc had been revealed. By 1820 AD Hans Christian Oersted - a Danish Physicist had discovered that an electric current is always accompanied by a magnetic field. In 1831 an English scientist

Michael Faraday wanted to see if the reverse would be true, that is, if a magnetic field would be accompanied by an electric current. Faraday moved a wire within the field of a magnet and saw that an electric current flows through the wire. This phenomenon came to be known as electromagnetic induction, and this principle is now used in the operation of electric generators and dynamos. Faraday died before he could do any further work on the connection between electricity and magnetism.

The connection between electricity and magnetism was later taken up by James Clerk Maxwell - a Scottish Physicist. He found that electricity and magnetism were alternate expressions for the phenomenon known as electromagnetism. He proved this by producing intersecting electric and magnetic waves from a simple electric current. James Maxwell expressed this mathematically in four linked equations which he presented to the Royal Society in 1864. These equations are now collectively known as Maxwell's equations and they showed that electric and magnetic waves travel at a speed close to that of light. From this he concluded that light itself is a form of electromagnetic wave. He also suggested that electromagnetic waves of different wave lengths may also exist and this was verified in 1887 by Heinrich Hertz - a German Physicist when he produced man made radio waves. There was further confirmation of James Maxwell's theory in 1895 with the discovery of X-rays.

James Maxwell also worked on the behavior of gases which was a continuation of studies by earlier scientists like James Joule who in 1840 discovered that heat is a result of the movement of molecules. This was the beginning of a new discipline known as thermodynamics. Earlier Joule had studied the movement of gas molecules and their speed, but found they varied greatly due to collision with other molecules. When James Maxwell took up these studies he concentrated on the probable distribution. The application of probability to molecular activity was revolutionary and James Maxwell presented his theory in 1866 and it came to be known as Maxwell Boltzmann kinetic theory of gases. Boltzmann was a scientist from Austria who independently reached the same conclusion in 1866.

James Maxwell also researched on how we perceive color. Earlier Isaac Newton had established that there were seven basic colors from which many combinations of colors can be produced. Thomas Young, another scientist in 1801 used spinning discs to show that our eyes recognize only three basic colors, those are green, red and violet. This was later modified by David Brewster to red, green, and blue and it came to be known as Trichomatic Theory of Colors. In 1860 James Maxwell presented a paper entitled 'On the Theory of Color Vision'. In this paper he conclusively proved the accuracy of the 'Trichomatic Theory of Colors' and showed that color blindness is due to the inability of a person to recognize red light. All the works taken up by James Maxwell that is electromagnetism, molecular behavior of gases, the color theory, were all ground breaking works, because they enabled the development of many of today's Technologies.

Now that the truth about the earth and its nature, and its position in the galaxy have been worked out variously by different Researchers, and the information about different life-forms have been collected, classified and identified, as well as their mode of inheritance have been determined, what remains is, the evidence about the position of the humans in relation to other life forms, and how the identity of each is maintained.

History of the origin of humans is best studied through fossils available in different layers of rocks. The records of the earth and the changes it has gone through such as changes in climates, changes in land masses, changes in flora and fauna, and finally the appearance of humans on earth and their early struggles are all available in the form of fossils in different layers of rocks. Geologists have divided different layers of rocks into eras, and each era into periods extending to several millions of years, and each period into epochs. The uppermost layers of rocks would be the closest to the recent times, and is known as the Cenozoic era. It consists of two periods -the Quaternary and the Tertiary periods. The Quaternary period is subdivided again into two. The first is known as Holocene which was followed by the last glaciations. These upper most layers of rocks are 1.5 to 65 million years of age. The Tertiary period is also subdivided into a number of sub periods, that is, Pliocene which represents 7 million years, Miocene represents 26 million years, Oligocene represents 38 million years, Eocene 54 million years, and Paleocene 65 million years. Below the Tertiary period starts the Mesozoic era consisting of three periods and those are Cretaceous period of 135 million years, Jurassic period of 190 million years, and Triassic period of 225 million years. Still lower layers of rock are known as Cambrian period rocks. All subsequent periods come under Paleozoic eras. In the pre Cambrian, Cryptozoic period is the lower most layer of rocks and is over 600 million years old.(Appendix 1)

The fossil records start appearing from the pre Cambrian times as unicellular organisms resembling bacteria and blue green algae in deposits dating back more than three billion years ago. In

Cambrian rocks which are about 570 million years of age, in addition to algae, a great variety of aquatic invertebrate animals started appearing along with some micro organisms and fungi. In the Ordovician period which is above that of the rocks of the Cambrian period, fish like vertebrates started appearing. In the Silurian period rocks, some primitive land plant fossils started appearing, along with spores with various markings of different land plants. Colonization of land plants was an event of enormous importance in evolution, because it made it possible for evolving animals to use them as food.

By late Devonian period, that is about 395 million years ago, arthropods including insects were established on land, along with the first terrestrial vertebrates, that is the amphibians such as frogs started making an appearance. In the plant kingdom, club mosses, horsetails, and ferns many of them tree-like unlike later ones, became abundant. Gymnosperms, mosses, liverworts, algae and fungi, began showing up in abundance. They provided a rich flora in the carboniferous period 345 million years ago.

In the Mesozoic era which consists of three periods starting from down upwards was the Triassic period of 225million years, Jurassic period of 190 million years, and Cretaceous period of 135 million years. This was the era of Dinosaurs of the animal kingdom, and Gymnosperms like Equisetales, Fillicales, Lycopodiales and Coniferales of the plant kingdom. Also trees like Cycas, Ginkgo, Silagenella, Horsetails and tree ferns were the dominant vegetation of the Triassic and Jurassic periods. Angiosperms that is, the flowering trees started appearing in the Jurassic period and became increasingly dominant towards the Cretaceous period. Soon some of the gymnosperms, tree ferns, and cycads began to decline and became lesser and lesser in number, and Angiosperms became the dominant plant group as it is today.(Appendix 1, 2A, 2B) This period also saw the extinction of the Dinosaurs, and the ascendancy of the mammals and the appearance of the early human forms. The humans of those days looked very different from the present day humans. The earliest fossil evidence of humans found so far are at Piltdown in Sussex UK, at Trinil in Java, and at Heidelberg in Germany, where human remains such as the top of the skull some teeth and thigh bone, and a smashed skull were found. In 1908 a skeleton of a Neanderthal man was found in a cave in Le Mousier in southern France.

In the prehistoric periods of the earth's evolution, some life-forms were profoundly affected, and in some cases became completely extinct, due to tremendous changes in temperature. There were cold periods four or five in number so far, known as ice ages, which were fatal to many life forms. These were always preceded or succeeded by sun ages. These climate changes did not extend throughout the entire world all at the same time, so that in ice ages animals migrated to places with warmer climates. But there were continental drifts when land masses got separated and flowing rivers went underground, leaving the ground barren and uninhabitable. Extinction of life-forms has been happening even before the advent of man on earth. It seems to be an inevitable phenomenon of nature, connected with the increase in consciousness and awareness of different life-forms to shed a given form and adopt a higher form more suitable to meet the challenges of the changing environment such as climate changes, and rearrangement of land masses. So it seems a waste of resources to identify endangered species and attempt to preserve them.

The most significant finding of the twentieth century is the discovery of the DNA as an individual's identity. It was the pioneering work of a German scientist called Friedrich Miescher on nucleic acids that was the first step to further research, which brought to light many facts regarding the chemical composition, structure, and other physicochemical characteristics of the nucleic acids. In the beginning itself they found that there were only two types of nucleic acids, one of which contained deoxyribose as one of the constituents and hence the name deoxyribonucleic acid (DNA), and the other contained ribose as one of the constituents and hence was called ribonucleic acid (RNA). In the beginning it was believed that nucleic acids from animals were DNA and from plant sources it was RNA. Later it was found that both DNA and RNA were present in all cells of both animals as well as plants. It is now known that a cell contains at least four classes of nucleic acids, that is, one DNA and three types of RNA. (Appendix 5)

Nucleic acids from all sources are compounds with high molecular weights. Most DNA has molecular weights ranging from 10^6 to 10^9 or more. RNA has much lower molecular weights. However the smallest of RNA has molecular weights of the order of 25000. When the nucleic acids are heated with strong acids or dilute alkali or treated with specific enzymes, they degrade into small molecular weight compounds which are classified into three groups (1) nitrogenous bases (2) sugars (3) Phosphoric acid. The nitrogenous bases found in DNA are adenosine, guanine, cytosine, and thymine. Some DNA samples contain 5-methylcytosene or 5-hydroxymethylcytosene in small amounts. Though RNA also contains four nitrogenous bases, thymine is replaced by uracil. These bases are broadly divided into two classes: purines and pyrimidines. A purine is a dicyclic compound containing a total of nine atoms in the ring. A pyrimidine is a monocyclic compound containing six atoms in the ring. Adenine and guanine are purines, while the others: thymine, uracil, cytosine, methylcytosin and hydroxymethylcytocine, are pyrimidines. The sugars found in nucleic acids are D - ribose and deoxyribose, of which ribose is found in RNA and deoxyribose is found in DNA. The basic units which when linked together form the nucleic acid are called nucleotides. A nucleotide consists of a base, a sugar moiety, and phosphate group. In DNA and RNA the nucleotides are linked together to form long linear molecules. If the phosphoric acid group is removed from a nucleotide the resulting compound is termed as nucleoside. The common nucleosides are adenosine, guanosine, cytidine, uridine, and thymidine. The term 'deoxy' is used to denote deoxyribonucleosides. In the case of thymidine the term 'deoxy is not used as it is found only in DNA. Both DNA and RNA are polymers of deoxyribonucleotides and ribonucleotides respectively. The works of several researchers have established that the nucleotides are linked together through phosphoric acid which forms phosphodiester bonds between sugar molecules. This type of linkage is repeated in the entire molecule, so that there is a kind of regularity in the structure (Appendix 5). Chemical studies of DNA from different sources have established that it consists of giant molecules with a molecular weight of over million or more, containing the four types of nucleotides linked together in long linear chains. By middle of the twentieth century it was established that DNA was the hereditary material and several researchers were attempting to study the nature of the chain. The methods used for the study was mainly through X-ray diffraction pictures of crystals of DNA.

The composition of the DNA from different sources was studied by extensive chemical analyses, and it was observed that the molar quantity of the base adenine was equal to that of thymine, and the molar proportion of guanine was equal to that of cytosine, and X-ray patterns also appeared to support this, because Watson and Crick saw that adenine must be linked to thymine, and guanine must be linked to cytosine so that all the bases exist in pairs, and they are held together by hydrogen bonds. Watson and Crick built a model in the form of a double helix or spiral with the two molecules entwined in opposite directions. The structure looked exactly the same whichever end was turned up. (Appendix 5).

The intertwined double helix looks like a spiral staircase. It has been calculated from X-ray data that one complete turn of the helix consists of ten nucleotide pairs 34 Angstroms in length. The diameter of the helix is about 20 Angstroms. The shape of the nucleotides - (that is the stereo chemical arrangement of atoms), the inter atomic distances, and the chemical composition of DNA (that is A=T and G=C) perfectly fitted the double helix proposed by Watson and Crick. The pairing had to be always between A and T, and between G and C, a large purine with a small pyrimidine. It was impossible to pair the bases together in any other combination. The bases fitted only when the phosphate- sugar chains were helically arranged and the orientation of the two chains was in opposite directions. This indicated that the chains had opposite polarity. It is the regularity in the polynucleotide chain that is at the root of the base pairing. The most remarkable feature of the structure was that it met the requirements for self reproduction of the gene.(App 5)

Research is still being carried out on DNA and researchers believe that they have found a second code in DNA in addition to the genetic code. The genetic code specifies all the proteins that a cell makes. The second code is reported to be superimposed on the first, and sets the placement of the nucleosomes (miniature protein spools around which the DNA is looped). The spools protect and control access to the DNA itself. The discovery is expected to open new insights into a higher order control of the genes, as for instance the process by which each type of human cell is allowed to activate the genes it needs but cannot access the genes used by other types of cells.

There are about 30 million nucleosomes in each human cell. So many are needed because the DNA strand wraps around each one only 1.65 times in a twist containing 147 of its units, and the DNA molecule in a single chromosome can be up to 225 million units in length. Biologists have suspected for years that some positions on the DNA, notably those where it bends most easily might be more favorable for nucleosomes than others. Eran Segal of the Weizmann Institute in Israel, and Jonathan Widom of North Western University in Illinois and their colleagues analyzed the sequence at some 200 sites in the yeast genome where nucleosomes are known to bind, and discovered an emerging pattern. This enabled them to predict the placement of 50 percent of nucleosomes in other organisms.

It may be noted that truth is never revealed as a whole. Scattered evidences have to be put together like in a jig saw puzzle to get the whole picture. This is not just an academic exercise. It is an exercise to understand the complexities of life, and how things have to go step by step from the very simple to the most complex, and this is a changing ever growing world because change is a part of growth.

REINCARNATIONS - THE INITIAL STEP IN EVOLUTION

O NE of the mysteries of life is how the different life-forms have been changing from one form to the other with the passage of time. In the beginning, before humans gained awareness and knowledge, and began wondering about their relationship with other life-forms, everything was taken for granted, as part of nature. But as geologists began studying rocks in order to estimate the age of the earth, they saw fossils of different life-forms appearing. In the upper layers, the forms that appeared resembled the ones that were present in the modern days. When they went deeper, they saw the fossils of trees and also some animals were very different from those of present days. As they went still deeper, they realized that they were now looking at the progress of life-forms, from the time they started. Though they started counting the age of the rocks from the top downwards, and divided them into eras and periods consisting of millions of years, they arranged the life-forms, from down upwards, because the lower levels contained the earlier life-forms some of which had now become extinct. The earliest life-forms, that is in the deepest layers of rock, seemed to consist of single cells even as they exist today. It is the largest forms like the Dinosaurs and giant trees and tree ferns, which appeared in the middle layers of rock that seemed to have vanished completely. The earliest forms of humans also from the relatively upper layers seem to have disappeared. The early humans though they walked on two feet and had arms and hands to work with, looked and behaved very different from modern day humans.

So it was concluded that life- forms first started as unicellular organisms such as prokaryotic cells when one unit of energy combined with one unit of matter. The life-form was then a mere energized matter in the form of plasma without any cell membrane or any chromosomes or genes. These prokaryotic unicellular organisms reincarnated into eukaryotic unicellular organisms with the passage of time. Each of these had a cell membrane surrounding it, and a tiny gene which was just a molecule of nucleoprotein, This must have happened when consciousness increased in the prokaryotic unicellular life-forms sufficiently for them to become aware of the potentials of their own bodies to produce a gene which would manufacture a cell membrane and give each cell an identity of its own.

In the beginning, when prokaryotic life-forms were created, there were several such life-forms which may be regarded as the first generation life-forms, and symbolized as A_0 , B_0 , C_0 , D_0 , E_0 , F_0 , G_0 etc. Each of them contained a number of inherent good and inherent evil traits. Each of them then multiplied by cleavage divisions such as for instance, A_0 multiplied into $A_{0.1}$, $A_{0.2}$, $A_{0.3}$, $A_{0.4}$, $A_{0.5}$ etc which could be regarded as the second generation life-forms. Similarly all the other life-forms also multiplied by cleavage divisions such as B_o into B_{01}, B_{02} etc and C_o into C_{o1} C_{o2} C_{o3} etc making an enormous amount of second generation life-forms. It may be noted that the parents as well as the offspring would also keep their separate individuality, and identity, and differ from each other based on the proportions of latent traits of good and evil in them, and evolve as separate groups of individuals undergoing different experiences. The next step to make the third generation life-forms would be, where the individuals of each generation combine with each other such as for instance, A_0 with B_0 forming A_0B_0; and A_{o1} with B_{o1} forming $A_{o1}B_{o1}$; and so on, in different combinations till each life-form gets bigger and bigger, and contain more and more traits, and sometimes more of a particular trait than the others. It is at this stage that the prokaryotic life-forms reincarnate into the eukaryotic life-forms. These life-forms are different from prokaryotic life-forms in that they now contain a tiny gene each, as well as a cell membrane.

From here onwards several generations of eukaryotic cells develop and live together in colonies. The method by which one type of life- form reincarnates into a more complicated life-form seems to happen, when the energy that pervades the whole body of the organism increases in consciousness and awareness, of the chemical structure of its own body, to manufacture a tiny gene and a cell membrane. These eukaryotic unicellular forms are now at a stage when inherent traits within different life-forms come together in a given life-form. This results in increase in size, as well as increase in consciousness and awareness of the energy that pervades the life-form. Also the different traits get redistributed in the offspring when the life-form reproduces itself by cleavage divisions, after combining with other life-forms.

In the next stage of reincarnation, each cell develops a number of organelles within itself, so that now each cell is a cell system; that is, it now consists of a nucleus with a nucleolus containing chromosomes and genes in the centre, and scattered in the surrounding cytoplasm are the mitochondria, ribosome, lysosomes, endoplasmic reticulum, Golgi bodies etc. all bounded by cell membrane of a complicated nature, each with a particular function to perform. These organelles are made up from the elements which compose the body of the unicellular organism, such as hydrogen, oxygen, carbon, nitrogen and phosphorus in various combinations, making up proteins, carbohydrates, and various types of lipids. The genes which are also a type of proteins exist as ultra microscopic particles which play a fundamental role in determining the nature of all cell substances, cell structure, and cell activities. So now the increase in consciousness and awareness of the energy that pervades the whole body, expresses itself in creating a system, whereby the identity of each individual group of life-forms can be maintained through chromosome numbers, and chromosome structure. This was a great stride forward in the evolution of life-forms.

Studies in cell biology have shown that an intercellular recognition system exists among each cell of a multi cellular body. Whereas in unicellular organisms, cells interact with each other at random during reproduction and colony formation; in multi cellular organisms, contiguous cells of the same organs interact with each other in the normal course of growth and development. These interactions take place through chemical and physical signals within the organism itself. Interacting cells of a particular organ of a given species, behave in their own characteristic ways as though they are programmed to transmit and receive special signals. Yet another feature of cells in multi cellular organisms is their cognitive properties. During embryo formation for example, cells make coordinate movements in cell formations of organs and distribute themselves to precise patterns. Just how this happens can only be explained by increase in consciousness and awareness of the energy which pervades the whole multi cellular organism. It may therefore be presumed that evolution of life-forms is really the result of the evolution of the soul, because in the beginning there is only consciousness which gradually develops into awareness, and later, awareness becomes knowledge, wisdom, and sensitivity, and then the soul is fully developed, consisting of three parts that is, the mind, the subconscious, and the aura. At the early cellular stage, there is only awareness of the self, at which time the soul consists of only consciousness at the initial stages of awareness and its role as an individual, in a particular group. At this stage, as the soul is not fully developed; it cannot be referred to as the soul. The next stage appears to be the grouping of the inherent traits present in the multi cellular mass to give it body forms with more or less similar traits.

It may be noted that evolution of life-forms by reincarnation is quite different from genetic evolution. Further, for the body to become, more complex in structure, the energy that pervades the whole body must first grow and get differentiated into three parts, that is the mind which is the seat of consciousness, the subconscious which is the store house of memories of experiences and reactions to different situations, and different talents developed in the various reincarnations that the given individual has gone through, and finally the aura which is the energy bag surrounding the individual. A fully formed aura is found only in humans, where it is the seat of all emotions, and which is plugged into the individuals at various points in the body. Aura is the area where the latent good and latent evil dwells. It is from here that they germinate, and grow into good or evil spirits, depending on the individual's reactions to different situations. The evil spirits generally enslave the individuals and make them commit crimes, while the good spirits try to restrain the individuals from going towards evil and self destruction. The good spirits in the aura, in common parlance is known as conscience.

There seems to be some evidence of the existence of the aura with its good and evil spirits, because there are reports in literature, where people have been guided by an inner voice. For instance Dr Lipton in his book on Biology of Beliefs reports "I heard an undeniable inner voice informing me that I was leading a life based not only on the false premise that genes control biology, but also on the false premise that we end, when our physical bodies die." What Lipton heard was probably the voice of the good spirit, the spirit of knowledge in his aura. It could easily be true when we consider that an individual is made up of a body and a soul. The body being made up of matter (which is another form of energy as compressed elements), cannot be annihilated; it can only change its form or go back to its original elements. The soul too cannot be destroyed or annihilated as it is made up of energy. So when an individual dies the soul cannot go back and join the original latent energy which makes up latent life, as it has gained awareness and knowledge through its different reincarnations, and hence is different from the latent energy of life that pervades the universe.

So the only thing that can happen to the soul is, to combine with its complementary matter again, and go through the whole process of development to get a new form in a different space and different time to undergo a different syllabus of experiences. This is reincarnation, and the purpose of reincarnation is for the soul to get new exposures in each incarnation and learn to cope with new situations, and in the process get rid of negative traits by gaining awareness of one's own shortcomings. So what Dr Lipton heard through an inner voice, 'that we do not come to an end when our physical bodies die', is correct. Further, that he was under a false impression that genes control biology was also correct; because, before the chromosomes and genes developed fully, the inherent traits within a unit of life had created a suitable body form for itself that would take it through several syllabi of experiences, for its further growth through reincarnations. The aim of reincarnations at the stage of lower life-forms seems to be to find ways of getting rid of all physical restrictions. So immobile life-forms devised ways of becoming mobile, in the plant kingdom by developing roots and rhizomes and seed structures that could be disseminated far and wide to develop colonies; and in the animal kingdom by developing different organs, such as fins and wings and limbs that would enable them to carry on many more different activities than just hunting for food as in the plant kingdom. After centuries, when they evolved into the human form, they had got rid of all the physical restrictions, and built up the consciousness in the ring of energy around the brain to enable them to think of ways to swim, fly, and travel great distances, without the body structures found in animals. In the human form, evolution was centered on development of abstract traits like further increase in consciousness, awareness, gathering of knowledge, development of reasoning powers, and inventing instruments for survival, wisdom, and sensitivity through several more reincarnations. In the process, they learnt to discern between good and evil when they are manifested as actions. Therefore it is the inherent traits in us, and our reactions to our different experiences that control our biology.

The evolution of life-forms by reincarnations is different from that of genetic evolution; firstly because in the former, (that is evolution by reincarnations) grouping is based on more or less similar inherent traits which were present originally when one unit of energy combined with one unit of matter. For instance all units of life which have a combination of abstract traits like fierceness, friendliness, protectiveness, and loyalty, as dominant traits may be grouped together in dog form as canines; while those that have a highly independent nature, and love wandering and exploring, and are fiercely conscious of their own territories and are possessive in nature, may be grouped together in cat form as felines and so on. Thus different combinations of abstract traits result in the formation of different animal groups.

Each group may contain a lot of variations within the limits of its form, depending upon proportions of different inherent traits, as for example, the feline group contains variations, from domestic cats to tigers, panthers, cheetahs, lions, leopards etc. Similarly canine group contains variations, from domestic dogs to wolves, jackals, foxes, hyenas etc. These are different lines of evolution depending on some latent dominant traits within each group. So, it would seem that the mechanism initially, in creation of different life-forms involves only the inherent traits present in the unit of life when it was first created. But as they evolve, they lose some traits and develop other traits which change their form when they reincarnate. So that may explain how some forms that became extinct like the dinosaurs reincarnated as humans, and some gymnosperms that became extinct reincarnated as angiosperms. It may therefore be presumed that it is the inherent traits that control biology rather than the genes. Genetic variations that occur are strictly restricted within the limits of the different lines of evolution within a given a group. It is these genetic manipulations through mating, hybridizations, or mutations in individuals within a group that produces different breeds of domestic animals and crops.

The Important differences between the evolution of life-forms through reincarnations and genetic evolution, are as follows:- In evolutions of life-forms through reincarnations there are (1) the group formations, based on inherent traits present initially in the life-form,(2) the functioning of the biological clock, which works for the group as a whole, so that each individual line of evolution within the group has (a) fixed life span,(b) fixed gestation period,(c) fixed overall body structure, and (d) fixed shapes of body at different stages of growth of individuals. Also at intervals there occurs the extinction of life-forms of a given group as a whole, or line of evolution as a whole within the group. These are not controlled by chromosomes. Whereas, the creation of the different groups, each with a particular type of body formation is dependent on the inherent traits within the original life-forms, the maintenance of these groups with their particular body formation is the responsibility of the chromosomes.

In the simpler unicellular life-forms like some bacteria, the life span is only 20 minutes. In the more complex forms, the life span runs into several years. Similarly, the gestation period of the more complex life-forms also vary from one group to the other. For instance in humans, the gestation period is nine months, while in dogs, cats, mice, sheep, birds, fishes etc all differ from each other and are much shorter. The changes of forms at different stages of growth are also more pronounced in humans than in animals; for example, an infant has quite a different form, from that of a child at the walking, speaking stage; and as time moves on, and the child becomes an adolescent, the form changes again. Later when the adolescent becomes an adult, the form and personality changes again, and last of all comes old age and senility as the time approaches for the soul to discard the body. The regularity, with which these changes take place in all the life-forms within each group, happens in a systematic and prescribed manner, which indicates a biological built in clock which cannot be seen, as it is not present as an organ. There is very little information available on this aspect as not much research seems to have been done on the actual mechanism involved. However it may be presumed that these biological clocks are physiological processes that work according to a prescribed time.

Now the question is, prescribed by whom? It is here that we get evidence of the fact that all life-forms are gaining awareness from within, starting from awareness of space and time, and this goes on throughout life at every stage of the life-form. It may also be presumed that the change from a multi cellular mass of cells to a given shape of life-form is visible evidence of the process of reincarnation based on the inherent traits present in the life-form initially. Each line of evolution within a group of life-forms then gets a fixed chromosome number, chromosome structure, and gene content, which controls their physical traits and their multiplication, mutation, and production of variations and their inheritance during reproduction. Chromosomes and genes however do not control inherent abstract traits like emotions, potential talents etc. Taking these facts into consideration, it would seem that in all life-forms there are two lines of control, one based on inherent traits which are interplay of emotions, potentials developed by the individuals in different reincarnations, and the opportunities provided by the environment. The other line of control is the chromosomes, genes, and environment responsible for causing physical changes within a given life time of an individual. Changes can also take place in a population by mating, involving parents and progenies and different generations. This is all about groups, while reincarnation is about changes in an individual with the passage of time.

A study of Paleontology (that is a study of fossils from stratified rocks) reveals a picture of life-forms as they existed in the past. Some of these indicate as is generally supposed, the 'ancestry' of the animals that exist today such as for instance in horses, camels, elephants etc as well as some animals up to the stage when they have become extinct for example Tetanotheres a prehistoric animal . If, as it is supposed, it indicates 'ancestry', then it should involve genetics. But that is not the case, because the changes involve the whole group, and not just individuals in the group as would be the case if genetics was involved. So the only plausible explanations for these changes that have taken place are that they [these changes] have taken place in different reincarnations of the individuals and not in the progeny as in genetic evolution.

The most extensive studies however have been done on the 'ancestry' of the horse, because a large number of fossils were available starting from the Eocene Period which was 54 million years ago. So with a series of fossils of the 'ancestor' of the horse available, it was possible to study the gradual changes that have been occurring with the passage of time. The so called 'ancestor' of the modern horse was a small animal that had four toes on its front legs instead of the single toe with a large hoof present in the modern horse. The changes which took place were very gradual starting with the reduction in the number of toes initially from four to three in the early Oligocene period, till finally it became one, in the Pliocene period. There was also an elongation of the leg bones starting from the late Oligocene period and ending in the Pliocene period. In addition, there was the formation of an extra joint in the leg bone. Further, there were changes in the teeth which gradually changed from the low crowned chewing type to the high crowned grinding type. The abundance of these fossils indicated that large herds of these animals roamed about in the land mass which now forms North America. All the changes that had taken place in the evolution of the horse have been directed towards achievement of speed of movement. So only those individuals from any group, that had speed as an inherent trait within it could reincarnate into this group.

There is still another example of the evolution of the life-form by reincarnation in the now extinct Tetanotheres which resembled the modern hippopotamus. It had four main lines of evolution, and in all of them the body grew into a bulky size, and all of them had a V shaped horn at the end of the nose. All four lines could be traced to a relatively small 'ancestor', who lacked the horns. But members of each of the four lines developed the V shaped horns simultaneously. Researchers put this development, as due to an 'inner tendency' in the original 'ancestor'. It may be noted that an inner tendency can arise only if there are inherent traits that can reincarnate and join a group.

Though fossils are valuable in giving us a step by step view of changes that have taken place in a given life-form through millions of years, the mechanism involved is not known, and the question that comes into the mind is, could all these changes which occurred simultaneously in all the members of a whole group be due to mutations? That is hardly likely. There has to be another explanation for changes that occur in the whole group simultaneously, and that can only be due to desire combined with increased consciousness, awareness, and knowledge of the potentials of the energy pervading the entire body which has been termed so far, as 'inner feeling' in the concerned life-forms. It is this increase in consciousness, awareness, and knowledge that results in reincarnation. This then is the mechanism by which reincarnation takes place; that is when a soul which has separated from its body at death in a given incarnation looks for a group of life-forms which has complimentary characteristics to itself where it can join, grow, and develop.

The main disciplines of biology which support the theory of reincarnations are comparative anatomy and embryology. For instance, comparative anatomy of the forelimbs of the horse, and the arms of humans, show a number of similarities. But interpretations of these similarities are perceived in different ways by different people. Some people see them as vestigial organs. But we see them as beginnings of a line of evolution for the next reincarnation into humans.

Another example is whales which have no outward visible hind limbs, and yet vestiges of hind limbs under the skin have been observed in them. This also we consider as the preparations for the next reincarnation as a terrestrial animal. These reported observations available in literature, along with our observations of some humans who show resemblances to horses, fish, rabbits, monkeys, ants etc in their facial structure, teeth formation, body language, and facial expressions, seems to us as though humans have evolved along multiple lines of evolution, rather than have arisen from mutation of chimpanzees. Further, the change from one form to a completely different form can take place, we feel, only with considerable increase in conscious awareness and knowledge of potentials of the self. It may take place in individual souls from possibly different groups in previous incarnations ,joining a group of life-forms that has complimentary characteristics to the soul that has just discarded its body of its previous incarnation.

The other discipline of biology, which supports the theory of the evolution of life-forms through reincarnations, is embryology. A study of embryology reveals that the human fetus starts out as a unicellular Being and divides itself first by cleavage divisions and repeats itself till it reaches the multi cellular stage. At this stage, each cell has become a cellular system capable of recognizing its own place in the particular life supporting system it belongs to, such as respiratory system, circulatory system, metabolic system, nervous system and reproductive system. Further development of the fetus, shows it undergoing different shapes, till it reaches the human form. So it is believed that each individual undergoes a repetition of its evolutionary history in the gestation period. Some more extensive studies seem necessary with proper sampling, taking into account the resemblance of the parents to any of the animal forms that the fetus resembles at different stages of its development to get a true picture of the whole situation. If a given unit of life has had several reincarnations as humans, the resemblance to animals is masked.

The evolution of life-forms through an 'inner feeling' is not really a new idea. It was first mentioned by Lamarck to account for inheritance of acquired traits. The idea was not acceptable at that time, because a large majority of people were under the impression, that all things were as God made them and remained unchanged. Anyone who differed from this idea was blaspheming and challenging God's authority. But as experimental science progressed, and found explanations for phenomena hitherto firmly rooted in the human mind, (as some things that are best taken on faith and left unquestioned,) began to change. Evolution was one such controversial subject. So people had to be wary as to what they believed, no matter what the observations were. It may be on this account that no one has so far attempted to explain the term 'inner feeing'. However a branch of genetics called Epigenetics does deal with adaptation of life-forms to environment due to 'inner feelings'. But the idea of life having begun with the arousal of consciousness was not known then. Hence it was termed as an 'inner feeling'.

In this book we have attempted to explain this 'inner feeling' as consciousness developing into awareness, which, in turn develops into knowledge with the passage of time. At the stage of individual cells, the awareness and knowledge gained is about being a part of a system which requires each individual cell to play its part efficiently without encroaching on others, and keeping to the allotted time and space, as well as to use the resources available within its Being, to manufacture its own organelles and keep them functioning. We have tried to show that evolution is the path taken by life-forms to gain this awareness in small degrees, till it is ready to be converted into knowledge and later into wisdom and sensitivity through several reincarnations at the human stage; because the objective of creating life-forms is to gain awareness, knowledge, wisdom and sensitivity and so be able to separate the good from the evil, as life has both inherent good and inherent evil in it. Moreover, the concept of reincarnations for the purpose of a progressive forward and upward movement provides an objective to creation of life-forms, and a direction to human lives. In any project, it is essential to have an objective, that is, the purpose to be achieved, without which it is impossible to decide the direction to be taken.

We have coined the term 'life-form' to include all creations, and have differentiated it from the word ' life' because there seems to be some confusion in the minds of some people who allege, that life can now be created in the laboratory, when they mean 'that building blocks of life-forms' can be made in the laboratory. Life itself has perforce to be completely abstract, as it is the Neutral Force that contains both the Positive Force [that is God] and the Negative Force [that is evil]. It is only the completely abstract things like 'life' that cannot be created or destroyed, and therefore has always existed and will exist for ever. In order to visualize 'life', we must know what it is made of; and the only things that we can think of that are completely abstract, and cannot be created or destroyed, and exist everywhere all at the same time, and are part of all life-forms, are :- space, energy and time. These three, are a trinity and have to work together,.

Some people believe that space and time are relative, and they do not exist. If space did not exist how would so many things exist in space? Also if time did not exist how would time manifest itself as parts of a day, as different seasons, as different stages of growth? But some Philosophers have concluded that space and time do not exist. As mentioned again and again in this book, a life-form is created when one unit of energy combines with one unit of matter, and that has to take place in a particular spot, at a particular point of time. Also as both energy and matter are indestructible, they can only change forms by being part of a changed life-form. Matter cannot be destroyed because it is a form of chemical energy made up of elements. The implication of this is that both energy and matter have to take on new forms which mean new reincarnations, so that with each new reincarnation, there are fewer limitations to the body and better facilities for progress; for example in the early unicellular stages there are no separate life supporting systems responsible for respiration, circulation, metabolism etc nor is there a nervous system which can help the life-form to perceive things better nor any sex differentiation. In each reincarnation, there is a step forward in the evolution of these different supporting systems as a result of increase in consciousness of the individual.

This chapter on reincarnation as the initial step in evolution was written specifically to clarify certain points brought out by

Dr Lipton in his book entitled Biology of Beliefs. These points are enumerated below as Lipton's quotes:-

Lipton's quote no. 1 "At first DNA was thought to be responsible only for our physical characteristics. But then we started believing that genes control our emotions and behavior as well. So if you are born with a defective happiness gene you can expect to have an unhappy life"

Lipton's quote no.2 "When we are convinced that genes control your life and you know that you had no say, in which genes you would be saddled with at conception, you have a good excuse to consider yourself as a victim of heredity. Don't blame me for my working habits - it is not my fault that I have been procrastinating on my deadline. It is genetic."

Lipton's quote no.3 "Since the dawning of the age of genetics, we have been programmed to accept that we are subservient to the power of our genes. The world is filled with people who live in constant fear that on some unsuspecting day their genes are going to turn on them".

Lipton's quote no. 4 "Lipton quoting Nijhout says 'genetic control has become a metaphor in our society. We want to believe that our genetic engineers are the new medical magicians who can cure diseases, and while they are at it, create more Einstein and Mozart as well. But metaphors do not equate with scientific truth".

From the above quotes, it may be seen how the whole situation of genetic manipulation can be misinterpreted, and fears created in the minds of people, who have overlooked the difference between the concrete which is the body having physical characteristics, controlled and manipulated by the chromosomes, genes and the environment, and the soul which has abstract characteristics like emotions and potentials. These abstract characteristics can only be changed by the attitude of the concerned individual, and what he or she learns from his or her syllabi of experiences in different reincarnations. Physical traits are inherited characteristics that come, some from the male parent and some from the female parent. So the offspring are not Xerox copies of either parent; but are a combination of both parents and therefore are separate individuals. Each individual also has his or her own inherent characteristics, which are abstract and control the attitudes and the perception of life. Both the physical characteristics as well as the inherent traits are modified to a great extent by the environment. These in turn influence the thoughts of the individual, and mould his or her attitude to life. This becomes apparent when one looks at pictures of ancient humans and compares them with modern ones. The facial expressions, body language etc differentiate the primitive from the modern, indicating how thoughts can bring about significant changes in expressions and indicate the level of evolution of the individual.

Reincarnation is a concept that is much misunderstood and misinterpreted probably because of its link with ancient religions. But in ancient times all life activities, and knowledge itself, were linked to religion. In modern times we hear occasional references to reincarnations or previous lives, in connection with any place or person that may seem familiar. So it may seem to some people, as a phenomenon to fulfill, unfulfilled desires. In the minds of some, it is also closely linked with the law of karma and a probable convenience to pay off old scores, or find an excuse to do some harm to someone and believe that they are merely paying off old scores.

But the main role of reincarnation seems to be in the evolution of the soul, and therefore the initial step in evolution of life-forms. After all, the beginning of everything is desire for self expression. The Bible says "In the beginning God said let there be light and there was light," and that was the first step to all creations one by one. This may be interpreted as the desire of space for self expression when energy came forth out of space, causing the initial awakening of consciousness when energy created the elements, which joined together to form the nebulae which then got separated into millions of stars, planets, satellites, and asteroids, each spinning on its own axis, and completing a whole circle in a fixed period of time. So now, consciousness has gone a step further to develop into awareness of time. From then on, awareness has developed step by step, from one reincarnation to the other; at first just awareness of time, awareness of space, awareness of self, to knowledge of a primitive type in the lower life-forms known as instincts. At each step, it is energy which is part of the life-form that is taking it to a higher and higher life-form till it has reached the human stage. So it may be presumed that it is consciousness that has gradually helped the soul to differentiate into a soul with three parts in the humans, who have relatively more complex structures than other animals, and hence the soul too has a more complex structure. But before reaching the human stage, the developing souls have had to reincarnate into different plant and animal forms depending on their inherent traits. At this stage however the developing souls cannot be termed as 'soul' because they are still at the stage of awakening consciousness. Some higher animals however, who are in touch with humans do develop a soul of more complex structure than their wild counterparts.

But so far, people have not paid much importance to the soul as such, having regarded it as some nebulous part, which does not play an active role in the life of the individual. This belief may be because so far, people have identified themselves solely with the body, with its life supporting systems which they can actually see. They have taken it for granted that these life supporting systems are a part of the body as it was meant to be, and it has not occurred to them that both the structure and the control mechanism of the life supporting systems of their bodies, were created as the soul increased in consciousness, awareness, knowledge, wisdom, and sensitivity. As such, health and well being of an individual can be traced to his or her soul. It must be recognized that everything physical starts from within. Even creation of life-forms started in the dim past when energy desired self expression. Many people find it difficult to visualize the effect of the mind upon the body. Yet all of us have observed the effects on our bodies when we hear some shocking unexpected news. In some, the face becomes pale and the body starts trembling; and some become dizzy or faint. In still other cases when you see a person with a drooping figure and dragging feet, you know that a failing state of mind is responsible for his failing condition of the body. Another case which many may have experienced is when they are angry their jaws become tight and they are unable to speak, or when they are sad they start crying. All these are physical effects of a mental state.

Ralph Waldo Trine in his book entitled 'In Tune with the Infinite' writes "Every thought tends to reproduce itself and ghastly mental pictures of disease, sensuality, and vice of all sorts, produce scrofula and leprosy in the soul, which reproduces them in the body. Anger changes the chemical properties of the saliva to a poison dangerous to life, and sudden violent emotions not only weaken the heart but causes death in some cases, and insanity in others." Further he writes about some scientific findings on the effect of the mind upon the body-"It has been discovered by scientists that there is a chemical difference between the sudden cold exudation of a person under a deep sense of guilt and the ordinary perspiration; the state of mind can sometimes be determined by chemical analysis of the perspiration of a criminal which when brought into contact with selenic acid produces a distinctive pink color, strong mental emotions often cause vomiting. Extreme anger or fright may produce jaundice. A violent paroxysm of rage is known to have caused apoplexy and death. Indeed, on more than one instance, a single night of mental agony has wrecked a life. Grief, long-standing jealousy, constant care and corroding anxiety sometime tend to develop insanity. ..."

FRAMEWORK OF COSMIC LAWS THAT RULE LIFE ON EARTH

B EFORE Isaac Newton's time, that is the 17th century, people had no idea that we lived in a world which operated within a framework of laws which could be predicted with mathematical precision. No one then had thought of connecting the way things moved, like falling of fruits from a tree, a bird flying, or a fish swimming, etc with the movement of the planets. Newton was the first one to show that every movement of anything on this earth or even perhaps in the universe behaves according to universal laws in orderly and predictable ways like a giant clockwork machine. In his book entitled 'Principia' he showed how every movement in the universe can be analyzed mathematically by the two branches of mathematics that he created and is now known as Differential and Integral Calculus. These branches of mathematics enabled the prediction of the simplest of every day movements performed by mankind to what would happen when a train goes across a new bridge or when a space craft is launched.

So Newton made it possible in theory to predict the movement of everything in the universe from the biggest star to the tiniest particle, mathematically.

Later, in the 19th century Einstein's discoveries showed a deeper subtler insight as to how universal laws work at extremes. His theory of relativity was so profound that it transformed the scientific view of space, energy, time, and matter. Some scientists believed that Einstein's ideas seemed to come out of nowhere, or maybe out of his own thoughts and reasoning. His theory of relativity gave a new explanation to gravity. Einstein himself described it as his disposition to abstract and mathematical thoughts. At the age of 26 Einstein was a clerk at a Swiss Patent Office. He held no university post, and had no access to a laboratory or academic library. But he kept contributing papers to a German Physics Journal called Annals of Physics. In 1905 he submitted five papers all of which were remarkable for their new ideas. One of them was an explanation for the photoelectric effect. Einstein explained that a beam of light was a stream of energy particles that he called photons. He said that when a beam of light hits a piece of metal, electrons are dislodged from the atoms on the surface of the metal. Photons with sufficient energy could knock electrons from their atoms. Although scientists were aware of the photoelectric effect, they had no idea how it was caused. They could not explain the fact when a beam of pure violet light is beamed on to a metal plate the plate ejects a shower of electrons. If light of lower frequency, such as yellow or red is beamed on the plate, the electrons will again be ejected but at reduced velocities. The power with which the electrons are torn from the metal depends on the color of light and not on its intensity.

If the light source is removed to a distance and dimmed to a faint glow the electrons that are torn out are fewer in number, but their velocity is undiminished. The action is instantaneous even when the light is very faint. Einstein felt that these peculiar effects could only be explained by supposing that all light is composed of individual particles of energy which he called photons. His line of argument was that high frequency radiation like violet and ultra violet photons pack more energy than red and infrared photons, and that the velocity with which each electron flies from the metal plate is proportional to the energy content of the photon that strikes it. Einstein used the recently developed quantum theory, and expressed these observations in a series of equations, for which in 1921 he received the Nobel Prize.

One of the papers submitted by Einstein for publication in the annals of Physics was entitled 'On the Electrodynamics of Moving Bodies'. This paper was about the Special Theory of Relativity which proposed that Space and Time are relative to the observer. Then the question arises as to why all of us perceive Space and Time in the same way. This was explained as due to the fact that we are all moving at the same speed relative to each other. An example given was "when the Observer and the Observed are at different speeds, as for example when a person standing on earth is observing a space ship travelling at a speed close to the speed of light, the space ship would appear to grow shorter. If it was possible for the observer standing on earth to measure the space ship's mass, he would find that it had become heavier. Also if he could compare the time on a clock in the space ship, he would notice that it was going slower than the clocks on earth. But the Astronomers on the space ship would see things differently. To them, the length and mass of the space ship, and the passage of time, would all seem normal as it originally was; and that is because they and the space ship are travelling at the same speed". The implication of this is that there is nothing called absolute space and absolute time. Both depend on the position and speed of the object observing them.

According to Einstein the only absolute thing is the speed of light which would remain the same where ever it is measured, and also nothing can go faster than light; because at that speed, an object would have infinite mass and no length, and time also would stand still. Further, to achieve this increase in mass, energy is needed to push the vehicle faster. This implies that energy has been turned into mass". Einstein then concluded that mass is really energy in a different form, in his famous equation $E=MC^2$ that means that energy is equal to mass multiplied by the speed of light squared. This is also supposed to explain how radiation worked and how a large amount of energy could be emitted by a small piece of radioactive material.

The contribution of Max Planck to our understanding of some universal laws pertaining to conservation of energy and radiation is very significant. He was born on 23rd of April 1858, and from an early age he was impressed by the idea that we live in a world controlled by absolute laws of nature. So he wanted to discover these laws. An opportunity came towards the end of his schooling when he learnt about the law of the conservation of energy, which is the first law of thermodynamics, and wondered if there were yet more to be discovered. So he decided to become a Theoretical Physicist and his decision was influenced by Rudolf Clausius's articles which introduced him to the significance of the second law of thermodynamics. This law dealt with the concept of entropy as a measure of disorder in a system that states, that in all natural processes of the world, entropy always increases. The example given is a hot cup of tea placed in a cold room soon loses its heat till it attains the temperature of the room. This is due to the difference in temperature of the room as compared to the cup of tea. This causes a flow of heat (a form of energy) from the cup to the room. Here a force has come into being to minimize the equilibrium of energy and maximize entropy. In 1897 Max Planck at the age of 21 obtained a doctorate degree from the University of Munich for his thesis on the second law of thermodynamics.

In 1888 Planck was offered a post of Associate Professor in the University of Berlin and in 1892 he was promoted to full professor there. Here he investigated how materials transform themselves from solid to liquid to gaseous states. He also studied electrolyses, which is the conduction of electricity through liquid solutions. By this study he found explanations for the laws governing the differing freezing and boiling points of different solutions.

In 1890 Planck became interested in the phenomenon of how heated substances radiate energy. He was aware that all bodies radiate heat at all frequencies, although maximum radiation is emitted only at certain frequencies which depends on the temperature of the body. Planck wanted to see if "Hotter the body, higher the frequency for maximum radiation" was true. Frequency is the rate per second of waves of any form of radiation. He wanted to see if this process was governed by a universal law. As hot bodies behave irregularly it was difficult to obtain accurate measurements of radiation and frequency in a laboratory. So he made use of a hypothetical object called 'black body' which completely absorbs and then reemits all radiation falling on it. He then studied the spectral energy distribution by plotting a graph showing how much radiation is emitted at different frequencies for a given temperature.

In 1896 William Wien working at the Centre for Radiation Research in Berlin suggested a formula that appeared to fit the spectral energy distribution worked out by Planck. In the following years Planck tried to make this formula fit in with his own theoretical experiments on the black body. In the meantime the measurements taken by the precession instruments at the Centre for Radiation Research showed that Wien's formula was valid only at high frequencies. It did not work for low frequencies. During this time two English Physicists Lord Raleigh and James Jeans arrived at another formula which was valid only for low frequencies and did not work for high frequencies. When Planck learnt about this discrepancy he started working on combining the two formulae to work at all frequencies. The new formula came to be known as Planck's Radiation Law. The formula that Planck worked out was expressed as $E = h v$ where v is the frequency of the radiation and h is Planck's constant, a very small but inexorable number consisting of a decimal point succeeded by twenty seven zeros followed by the number 6624. This has proved to be one of the most fundamental constants in nature. In any process of radiation the amount of emitted energy divided by the frequency would always be equal to h. Like all other universal constants, it is simply a mathematical fact which cannot be explained though it has dominated the computations of atomic physics since the beginning. The far reaching implications of Planck's law became apparent only when Einstein brought out its significance and postulated that all forms of radiant energy that is light, X-rays, and heat actually travel through space in separate and discontinuous quanta.

However, there are certain phenomena where light can only be explained by the wave theory. For example when a beam of light is passed through a round aperture, it projects a sharply defined disk upon the screen. If the hole is reduced to the size of a pinhole then the disk becomes ribbed with alternate concentric bands of light and darkness. This phenomenon is known as diffraction, and has been compared to the waves of an ocean when passing through the narrow mouth of a harbor they bend and diverge. If instead of one pin hole, two pinholes are placed very close together side by side, the diffraction pattern merge in a series of parallel stripes. These phenomena of diffraction and interference are known to be strictly characteristics of waves. Therefore if light is made up of only quanta in all situations, the diffraction and interference shown in the experiment above would not occur. So this fundamental question whether light occurs in all situations as waves, or in all situations as quanta, or in some as waves and some as quanta, remained to be solved.

This dual character of light is also observed to pervade other phenomena in nature. It was Louis de Broglie - a French Physicist who first suggested that the phenomena involving the interplay of matter and radiation is best understood if electrons are regarded as a system of waves, instead of individual particles. This was a revolutionary idea because up to this time, the electrons had been pictured as hard elastic spheres. It was shortly after Broglie had his idea of electrons being regarded as 'matter waves' that a Viennese Physicist called Schrodinger developed the same idea and put it in a mathematical form thus evolving a new system that explained the quantum phenomena by attributing specific wave functions to electrons. This system came to be known as 'wave mechanics'. This was corroborated in 1927 by two American Scientists called Davisson and Garner who proved by experiment that electrons do exhibit wave characteristics.

Davisson and Garner directed a beam of electrons on a metal crystal and obtained diffraction patterns analogous to those produced when light is passed through a pinhole. They used a crystal, because in a crystal there is an even and orderly arrangement of its component atoms, and a closeness of their spacing which would serve as a diffraction grating for very short wavelengths such as X-rays. Their measurement indicated that the wavelength of an electron is of the precise magnitude predicted by Broglie's equation that is $\lambda = h/mv^4$ where 'v' is the velocity of the electron, 'm' is its mass, 'h' is Planck's constant. Further experiments showed that not only electrons but whole atoms and even molecules produce wave patterns when diffracted by a crystal surface and their wavelengths are exactly what de Broglie and Schrodinger forecast separately.

It may be noted that earlier, the atom was pictured as a miniature solar system composed of a central nucleus surrounded by electrons, the number of electrons of which varied for different elements such as one for hydrogen, two for helium, and so on. Earlier experiments had indicated that all electrons had exactly the same mass and the same electrical charge so much so that they came to be regarded as the ultimate foundation stones of the universe. But when investigation progressed, the behavior of the electrons was observed to be too complex for them to be regarded as material particles, because a material particle has a definite position in space, which electrons apparently did not. So finally electrons are now visualized as an undulating charge of electrical energy and the atom has become a system of superimposed waves.

The paradox of waves of matter on the one hand and particles of light on the other was resolved by several developments in the decade before the Second World War. Two German Physicists Heisenberg and Bonn bridged the gap by developing a new apparatus that permitted accurate description of quantum phenomena both in terms of waves, and in terms of particles, according to a given situation. Bonn took the mathematical expression used by Schrodinger in his equations to denote wave function and interpreted it as a probability in a statistical sense. That is, he regarded the intensity of any part of the wave as a measure of the probable distribution of particles at that point, as for example in an ocean wave, its properties and intensity are indicated by the position of its crest and its trough, and the crest becomes more significant because it contains more molecules of water than the trough. So Bonn dealt with the phenomenon of diffraction which so far only wave theory could explain, in terms of the probability of certain quantum of light or electrons following certain paths and arriving at certain places. Thus waves of matter were reduced to waves of probability. These findings have an impact on the progress of our understanding of the role of light on the biological mechanisms of growth and development.

There is both visible and invisible light. The visible light is that part of the electromagnetic radiation spectrum which lies between violet (that is 380 nm) and red light (that is 750 nm). This range of light is the energy source on which plants depend for photosynthesis. Apart from acting directly as an energy source, the visible light may also have a regulatory role in the life of the plant for example the orientation of the plant with respect to light, as well as in daily timing of plant growth reactions.

Radiation must first be absorbed by a chemical substrate in order to enable it to produce an effect. The absorbing substrate in plants is the pigment systems which consist of chlorophylls, phytochromes, carotinoids, anthocyanins, and flavors. All these are used in precisely controlled ways. These substrates are molecules which contain a chromophoric group responsible for their colors. The particular color is caused by a given member of the chromophoric group absorbing only some wave lengths of white light, for example chlorophyll looks green because they absorb the red and blue parts of the spectrum, and transmit the green; while beta carotene appears orange because it absorbs the blue end of the spectrum and transmits yellow and red. The spectral quality of light, and intensity and duration of light, affects metabolism and development of plants in different ways.

Planck's quantum theory of radiation transfer comes into focus when we want to know what happens when a pigment absorbs light. We only know that a photoreaction takes place and this leads to energy conservation. But to know the actual mechanism involved we have to refer to Planck's quantum theory of radiation which states that transfer of radiation takes place in discreet packets of energy called quanta. The energy transferred (E) is related frequency of radiation (v) multiplied by Planck's constant, that is, $E = h v$ where h is the Planck's constant and v is the frequency of radiation.

Einstein used the term 'photon' for energy of a single quantum of light. The energy of a photon depends on the wavelength absorbed and frequency is inversely related to wavelength expressed as microns. So energy of the photon can be expressed as $E = hc/\lambda$ where 'c' is the speed of light ($3*10^8$ ms^{-1}). Then a photon of blue light 450 nm contains more energy than a photon of red light 650 nm. One mole of a compound absorbs N photons, having energy which can be represented by the formula $E = N h$ where 'N' is equal to $6.023*10^{23}$ (Avogadro's number). The total energy absorbed per mole is called an einstein (E). An einstein of red light has less energy than an einstein of blue light though both have the same number of quanta N.

Frequency is normally expressed as the number of vibrations per second. For example, when you drop a stone in a pond, a wave spreads out where the stone impacts water. If you drop more stones repeatedly, a number of waves are formed each at the point of impact. The faster the stones are dropped, the closer are the peaks of the waves together. The distance between the peaks of two waves is the wavelength. As the velocity of the propagation of the waves remain constant, the shorter the wavelength, the greater the frequency, that is when speed of propagation is divided by wavelength it will be equal to frequency. In the case of light we have to modify the equation describing energy of a photon with the expression $E = h c$ divided by λ where c is the velocity of light ($3*10^{10}$) centimeters per second. λ is the wavelength of light in centimeters. The actual value of h is $.6624*10^{-27}$ erg per second.

In biochemistry, the terms used are calories per mole of substance instead of ergs as a term and a variety of units are used for wavelengths of light. Radio waves are measured in meters or centimeters, visible light is measured in either mill microns or Angstrom units [1 meter = 10^2 centimeters, or equal to 10^3 millimeters, or is equal to 10^6 microns, or is equal to 10^9 milli microns. The Angstrom unit is 10^{-8} centimeters and is therefore equal to 1/10 of a mill micron]. By multiplying with the appropriate constants, the equation relating energy to a wavelength of light can be written as $E = 2.86*10^7$ calories per mole divided by wavelength in mill microns. A mole is equal to $6*10^{23}$ photons. Thus by making our energy calculations on this basis, we can speak of calories per mole as is done in ordinary chemical reactions. Blue light with a wavelength of 450 mill microns is equivalent to approximately 64 kilocalories per mole. It is then seen that different colors of light represent photons or quanta of different energies, for instance blue light has more energy than that of red light. Thus the connecting link between corpuscular and wave theory of light lies in the fact that the energy of photons is directly proportional to the frequency of light waves.

According to Lincoln Barnet there are at present two gateways through which we have to enter, to understand physical reality; one is the two hundred inch reflector of the Palomar Telescope on Palomar Mountain. The other gateway to our knowledge of the physical world is Einstein's Unified Field Theory. Today the outer limits of our knowledge are defined by the Theory of Relativity, and the inner limits by the Quantum Theory. The Theory of Relativity has shaped all our concepts of space and time and gravitation; the Quantum theory has shaped all our concepts of the basic units of matter that is the atoms and energy. These two systems are completely different and unrelated. The Unified Field Theory attempts to construct a bridge between the two theories. Einstein believed in harmony and uniformity of nature and tried to evolve a theory to encompass both, the phenomenon of space, and the phenomenon of the atoms. Although it may not have succeeded in achieving all that was envisaged by Einstein, it at least unites the laws of gravitation and the laws of electromagnetism within one superstructure of the universal law; not that the two laws are the same, but that the two are dependent on each other, and that they are in a physical sense inseparable.

Thus the various forces in the world as they are discovered one by one, seem to be different manifestations of the electromagnetic force; and all the different kinds of radiations that is, light, heat, X-rays. Radio waves, gamma rays are all just electro-magnetic waves of different wave lengths and frequencies. Lincoln Barnett believes that ultimately, the features of the universe boils down to basic quantities of space, energy, time, and matter, and also gravitation. Einstein in his special theory of relativity demonstrated that matter and energy are inter-convertible; and in his general theory of relativity he showed the indivisibility of space and time.

Apart from knowledge of physical laws that control life on earth, it is also of interest to have at least a basic knowledge of the process by which the continuance of the race was ensured. It is here that genetics plays an important role. In the beginning of evolution, reproduction took place by the cells multiplying themselves by cleavage divisions and asexual reproductions. In the course of evolution, special cells were developed for sexual reproduction, and it became necessary for two reproductive cells to combine for fertilization to take place. This change in the process is believed to have favored natural selection. So the two reproductive cells, that is the sperm and the ovum each contained half the number of chromosomes that the rest of the body cells contained, for example in humans, the chromosome number is 46 in the body cells, but in the sperm and the ovum of humans there are just half the number that is, 23 each; so that when they combine they would produce a body with 46 chromosomes. This is a mechanism to ensure that like begets like, because different animals differ in their chromosome numbers and chromosome structures.

Sex differentiation first originated in the chromosomes not only in humans, but also in animals, birds, insects, and plants. The chromosomes responsible for different sexes and present in the sperm and ovum, differ in appearance from the chromosomes found in the cells of the rest of the body. In the sperm, the two chromosomes that form a pair differ from each other in size, the bigger one is designated as X chromosome and the smaller one of the pair as the Y chromosome. On the other hand, the two chromosomes of the pair in the ovum are both of the same size, and larger than the chromosomes of the rest of the body, and are designated as X X. So the sexes are represented as XY for the male and as XX for the female. During the normal course of growth, the body cells are continuously multiplying in number, but at the same time maintaining the chromosome structure and the chromosome number of each cell of the given species; and this process is known as mitosis. When the reproductive cells have to be developed, the number of the chromosomes in the sperm, as well as the ovum has to be halved and this process is known as meiosis or reduction division. The fertilized ovum therefore may either be XX or XY having received one of the pair from the female and one of the pair from the male. The progeny with the

XX chromosomes then becomes a female, and the progeny with X Y becomes a male. However, the sex- chromosome formula is different in different life-forms. In some insects and some lower animals such as moths, butterflies, and birds the female is XY and the male is XX. Goldschmidt in 1901 suggested that every individual has genes for both sexes and that sex determination depends on the interaction of male and female genes in different proportions and this is known as Goldschmidt's theory of gene balance.

The theory that hereditary units are genes which are located on the chromosomes is known as the chromosome theory of heredity. The chromosome theory first came into focus shortly after the discovery of Mendel's principles in 1900. Bovary and Sutton in 1904 were among the first to recognize the parallelism in the behavior of the chromosomes and genes, and to suggest that genes are located on the chromosomes. At about the same time E.B.Wilson strongly advocated the chromosome theory on the basis of more or less the same evidence as that of Bovary and Sutton and that is (1) both chromosomes and genes occur in pairs. (2) The members of a pair of both chromosomes and genes segregate at reduction division. (3) Members of different pairs whether chromosomes or genes are assorted independently of one another. It is this parallelism which originally led to the conclusion that genes are located on the chromosomes. In 1906 R.H. Lock published a book called "Recent Progress in the Study of Variation Heredity and Evolution" in which the chromosome theory was summarized. In 1911 a team of geneticists Morgan, Bridges, Muller, and Stewart gave further evidence in support of the chromosome theory leading to its final acceptance. Mendel's contribution to the chromosome theory was that it was he, who originally showed how genes were distributed in heredity, and later biologists found that chromosomes were distributed in the same way. Thus Mendel's experiments laid the foundation for the chromosome theory.

So far we have dealt with laws concerning Mendelian genetics. Apart from this, there is also population genetics, the fundamental law of which is known as the Hardy-Weinberg law. This law states that gene and genotype frequencies in Mendelian populations would have remained constant generation after generation, if there were no evolutionary forces such as mutation, migration, genetic drift and selection. All these phenomena occur in nature spontaneously. To explain this situation, we must take for example a chromosome in which two alleles occur on a locus, i.e. (A) and (a). There would then be three genotypes, those are (AA), (Aa) and (aa). If 'p' stands for frequency of allele (A) and 'q' stands for frequency of allele (a), the frequencies of the three genotypes in a population can be represented as (p^2AA), $(2pAa)$ and (q^2aa). And the sum of 'p' and 'q' would be one, that is p+q =1. Such a population would be at equilibrium with respect to the given locus because genotype frequencies would not change from generation to generation. This equilibrium is known as Hardy-Weinberg equilibrium. Any change in the equilibrium is brought about by selections, mutations, migrations and genetic drifts.

An allele is any one pair of genes, or a series of genes, which is situated at the same locus in a chromosome. Allele genes may be made up of two correlated dominants, or two correlated recessives, or a mixture of one dominant, and one recessive gene.

Genetic drift only happens in small isolated populations. It pertains to the change in the genetic makeup of a population occurring by chance and not as a result of natural selection.

Natural selection is the chief mechanism of evolutionary change first suggested by Darwin in 1859. According to this theory, evolution occurs by a process known as natural selection from a range of different individuals that make up a population. Individuals in this population having certain characteristics that contribute more offspring to succeeding generations, and if these characteristics have a basis for being carried over to the next generation, the composition of the population gets changed. The theory of natural selection asserts that the contribution of the offspring to this generation is not entirely random, but is correlated with variability. Some variant individuals are consistently more successful than others in contributing offspring to future generations. The successful variants and their progeny are said to be 'selected' by a natural process.

Mutation is a sudden change in the chromosomal DNA. The most important mutations are those occurring in the gametes or their precursors because they can produce an inherited change in the characteristics of the organisms. These changes would be the basis for evolution. The majority of mutations is changes in individual genes and is known as gene mutations. Some mutations are caused by gross structural alterations in the chromosomes such as inversions and translocations. Sometimes changes in the number of whole chromosomes per nucleus may take place and this is termed as polyploidy. Mutations are generally a very infrequent event. But it can be artificially produced by irradiation with X-rays, gamma rays, neutrons, as well as some chemicals such as mustard gas. Evolution occurs by natural selection of mutations, and not by direct mutations. On the whole, majority of mutations are deleterious upsetting the balanced mechanism of embryonic development of the organism. Gene mutation takes place when there is a substitution of a nucleotide for an existing one in the DNA, which then alters the amino acid sequence of the protein normally dependent on the gene. This sort of change has a repercussion in the structure and function of the organism.

Gametes – is the combined term for the male and female reproductive cells that is, the sperm and the ovum.   When fertilization takes place, the nucleus of the sperm and ovum fuse along with their cytoplasm to form what is known as the zygote, which by repeated divisions forms a multi cellular mass which finally develops into the individual.

Genetic changes play a more prominent role in plants, insects, and lower animal forms. In humans, genetic changes are very rare and not so apparent as in the lower life forms. In humans, the changes caused by gene mutations are mainly in the form of diseases such as albinism, alkaptonura, galactosemia, hemophilia A, hemophilia B, hypophosphatasia, maple syrup urine disease, pentosuria, phenylketonuria, sickle cell anemia, and Wilson's disease. In all these cases it is either the absence of an enzyme necessary for a chemical reaction or a protein that is affected.

The laws of genetics and the laws of evolution are intertwined and interconnected. The laws of evolution which involves major changes in form are not based on genetics; such as, changes in the form of an individual at different stages of growth in humans. Yet chromosomes have the responsibility of the smooth running of the chemical reactions which produces the growth of the individual, though not the actual changes in form. Further, the changes in form from one reincarnation to the other, is entirely the responsibility of the growing consciousness of the soul. Here chromosomes and genes have no role to play. The two stages of evolution in an individual's life may be termed as (1) microevolution and (2) macroevolution. The former (that is microevolution) is the changes in form that takes place in an individual within a given lifetime, that accompany different stages of growth; such as from infant at the crawling stage, to the baby at the walking speaking stage, to adolescence, to adult, to old age and senescence. On the other hand, macroevolution takes place after the death of the individual, when the soul separates from the body with which it has grown up to a point, and now has to separate because the form of the body is finite, though the matter with which the body is made is indestructible, and disintegrates into the elements which composed the body. The soul now combines with a larger molecule of matter with which it can produce the required form for its next reincarnation. These different lifetimes that an individual's soul has to go through, to undergo different experiences to increase in consciousness and awareness and gather knowledge and develop wisdom and sensitivity, is similar to a child going to school and passing from one class to the other, and studying a different syllabus in each class. The aim of reincarnations is for the soul to be exposed to different situations in space and time in each reincarnation, till it awakens completely from its original latent state, to a state of full consciousness of what is good and what is evil by overcoming temptations and developing restraint and self control. But even after it has gone through all the prescribed reincarnations, it still has to undergo further training to immigrate into the spirit world.

According to some ancient Vedic Literature, when the souls of humans have reached the stage when they can be admitted into the spirit world, they are allowed into the first phase of heaven, where they have to undergo training to live and work as spirits, where there is no death, no changes in form, no sex differentiation, and no marriage, no scope of worry or unhappiness of any kind. In the next stage, the souls are nearer God and have to work in various capacities such as guiding and protecting and inspiring humans, keeping records and finding newer and more efficient methods of doing things, working out syllabi of experiences for all life-forms for their progressive reincarnations in space and time, analyze all the data recorded and interpret them, and revise laws as man gains more awareness, decide on the forms that have to be given to replace extinct forms etc. The third stage in the spirit world is where those souls that have graduated to become God-like are sent out into the world as Incarnations, Buddha, Prophets, Sages, Seers and Religious Teachers. It is only those souls that have passed this stage successfully and have overcome all temptations of various kinds that can become one with God to work with Him to keep down evil, and see that evil is never allowed to overcome the good. Others who have fallen by the wayside, or who have not made the grade, have to repeat more reincarnations by coming to earth in human form, till all weakness and all negative qualities are distilled out of their systems.

Apart from physical laws, genetic laws, and evolution laws, as given above, there are also some general laws that govern life on earth, such as the law of karma which is equivalent to Newton's third law of motion, and which states that every action has a reaction equal and opposite. This law has a very wide range of applications, especially on human behavior. The word karma has its origin in Sanskrit, and is a combined term for thought word and action and this term has been used here because there does not seem to be an equivalent in English. Every word and action has its roots in thought. Every action performed may be either a physical action or a 'word action'. But both have reactions which are equal and opposite. In its simplest form, in the law of karma the result of action performed is immediate, but in more complicated cases, the results may be delayed. Some examples of cases are given below:-

(1) A boy for the thrill of experiencing speed, bicycles down a hill side and loses control and comes crashing down and hurts himself. So his desire for experiencing the thrill of speeding without considering the consequences resulted in pain. That is action and reaction being equal and opposite with immediate effect.

(2) In another case, a child watching some ducks swimming in a pond thinks that a duck was never taught to swim and yet it swims pretty well, and so can I, and jumps into the pond and nearly gets drowned and has to be rescued. Here again, the action began with the thought and the result was immediate.

(3) In another case a bully in school enjoys himself dominating and terrorizing others. After a couple of years when he graduates out and looks for a job, he finds that no one wants him. As he cannot survive without employment he takes the first thing he eventually finds. His employer pays him much less than others

and makes him work overtime. He feels helpless and victimized but sees a mirror image of his own actions as a bully in school. So here again is a case of action and reaction being equal and opposite but with some delayed effect. This delay was a necessary factor in this case, because the law of karma is first and foremost a corrective measure, and the bully had to mature sufficiently to connect up his former action with what was happening to him currently. All these are cases involving physical action.

(4) In another case of delayed action, P who was a Liaison officer in an organization was demoted to the position of a secretary to the Director by the new Director. But as P had no knowledge of secretarial work and was over confident of her position in the organization, she felt she would be favored by higher-ups, and get her previous job back, and so made no effort whatsoever to learn and adjust to her new job. As a result she lost the job. Few years later, the same organization got reorganized and the same Director who had demoted P had to step down and was made deputy to the Chief Director. But he felt redundant in this post and so resigned and left the job. Here the Director got the reaction to his action after a delayed period of time. But P got the reaction to her action immediately, for not making an effort to learn and adjust to her new job. This is a little more complicated case than the first two cases as it involves two sets of people.

(5) In a still more complicated case, people who are slaves to evil spirits of jealousy, hatred, anger, resentment, and lust, soon find themselves helpless victims of their own actions, and they are unable to restrain themselves and apply any self control,

and drift through life with a sense of guilt which makes them restless and unhappy, which in turn, makes them want to make others unhappy. This is something that is happening to them from inside, and is far worse than being exploited from the outside by another individual. Further, they find that jealousy and hatred are emotions that ultimately cause painful diseases like high blood pressure, hypertension and migraine and in some cases even paralyses. The only solution to such a situation is to set apart some time every day for prayer and meditation and ask God to cleanse their aura of all evil spirits residing there. This is a case of action and reaction which involves thought and habits.

(6) Criminals performing crimes are unable to stop themselves as they are urged by the evil spirits that reside in their aura and so they live in a constant state of fear and worry and guilt, because they are slaves to these evil spirits and there is no way they can get away from them. This is another example where thoughts have become habits and have come under the law of karma. Here awareness of one's own shortcomings and an appeal to God for help is the only solution.

(7) On the other hand, people who have become aware of their own shortcomings and have conquered their ego, and have practiced, or at least attempted to practice discipline and self control and restraint, are constantly guided by the good spirits residing in their aura, and are ever protected by them. Even when they have to go through the worst of adverse circumstances they are not even aware of them, because they are supplied by God with an inner strength to listen to the good spirits in their aura,

who guide them step by step to solve the problem, and at the same time to learn the lessons that the adverse circumstances had to teach. Often God sends them outside forces to help them out, after they themselves have gone through all that they can do, and cannot do more. These sort circumstances also come under the law of karma, because it pertains to thoughts and attitudes.

(8) Another circumstance is where a habitual criminal steal, murder, rape, and torture victims, suddenly finds himself in a situation similar to the one he has made his victims undergo; because one morning he finds that he can neither talk nor move, and there is no one around to help him, and he is completely paralyzed. He was terrified and demoralized in the same way as all his victims were in the past. Someone finally came to help him to take him to hospital, and there he was treated with indifference and callousness which was a reflection of his own inner self, because the law of karma was teaching him the need to develop sensitivity. In some situations the reaction is not immediate as it involves the syllabi of experiences of many people, and so it may even take place in any of the next reincarnations.

(9) Once there was a couple who by instinct was benevolent and was ever present wherever help was needed. This couple kept an open house, not only for their own friends, but for people who lived alone and were lonely, or in need of temporary shelter. They went out of their way to give an open invitation to all such individuals who would like to share a meal and have some company, whenever they felt the need; or even to just sit in a corner of their garden to have some peace and quiet and spend some time

for reflection and meditation, or even to do some painting and writing. As this couple was never judgmental, and never criticized anyone, or found faults, people usually came and confided in them, and they would do all they could to help them without expecting any returns .This couple never had any security guards to guard their house and never closed their doors. They were never robbed even when there were thefts and burglary in their neighborhood. Here again is a reflection of the law of karma which does not involve just a single action, but involves a whole attitude where kindness and consideration for others and helping those in need, creates an atmosphere of happiness, harmony, peace, security, and goodwill.

(10) Another story is about a man who was from a poor background, and had to go out and earn his living even before he was a teenager doing miscellaneous manual jobs, to contribute to family finances. He however had a yearning for education and was helped by benevolent people of the neighborhood who pooled their resources and paid for his education through school and law college. Now this Mr X being a person with many evil spirits in his aura, fooled himself by thinking that now he had a career by which he could become all powerful. His victims were mostly people with vast properties, who all the same were ignorant of the laws pertaining to properties. He identified them, befriended them, and cheated them by various nefarious means using the knowledge of law that he had gained through his law degree. He put these properties in various people's names but kept the documents with himself along with the power of attorney from each; so that he had complete control over all of them. Then one

day he had a road accident in which his brain was injured and he had to be hospitalized for several months amounting to more than a year. The people from whom he had taken the power of attorney then went to the doctors attending on him, and got a certificate saying that his chances of recovery was very slim and even if he recovered there was no guarantee for his sanity. They then got an advocate to cancel all the power of attorney that he had obtained from them, and went to his office and got hold of all the property papers and sold all the old properties, and bought new ones in their names. Further they mortgaged his prime property to themselves, to pay for his hospital charges. Thus all the properties that he had obtained by nefarious means were lost. When he recovered, he found not only that he had lost everything, but that he was deeply in debt. So after a couple of years of deep humiliation and financial misery, he died a disappointed lonely man. Here although he got the reaction for his action, the law of karma had not yet finished with him. He still had to pay for the financial losses he had caused the people he had cheated. This could only be done in several reincarnations as it involved several people and their syllabi of experiences. In the current incarnation he had only seen a reflection of his own actions. It is in such cases that the results of one's action gets carried over to the coming reincarnations. So in his next incarnations he would have to return to each, to pay back what he had stolen from them, either by having to work under them for much less remuneration, or not receiving some of the allowances that he was entitled to; or even incur losses in any investments that he may make in his new incarnation, or he may be born into the very family he had ruined. The law of karma gets more and more complicated depending on the circumstances and the level of evolution of the concerned victims and their syllabi of experiences, for which, time and space have to match with the syllabus of each person concerned. All the same, the law keeps strictly to action and reaction being equal and opposite. Jesus who was a manifestation of God Himself, has demonstrated that this law is infallible, when He took the sins of others on Himself and paid for them on the cross.

(11) The next case is about a widow whose life centered on her only child - a daughter who she regarded as superior to everyone else. The widow was in the habit of maligning and running down all other girls in her neighborhood, so much so, people dreaded her visit to their houses. One day the widow's daughter came home with a friend and told her mother that a group of them were going on a historical trip for the week end. When she did not return after the week end, the widow went to the friend's house to find out what had happened. The friend told her that the historical trip that her daughter had referred to was her wedding, and that a group of them had gone as witnesses as well as to celebrate the event. This humiliation was more than the widow could bear, but it was a result of her own action in humiliating the parents of all the girls in the neighborhood. In this case the law of karma was dealing with a word- action and not with an actual physical action.

(12) There was a man who was an introvert and kept strictly to himself even while he was in service. But he had a kind and caring disposition, and helped all those who came to him seeking for help without expecting any gratitude. But he himself never visited anyone, and never invited anyone, although all who visited him

was made welcome. This man never lacked company because children and animals flocked to him and they made themselves comfortable in his house. The children brought their pets to his house to help them groom the pets, or to just talk to their pets about good behavior. They also got him to help them with their home work, and chatted to him about their school activities, their teachers, their friends, their families, their ambitions, and their problems. The older boys who loved talking politics brought their friends for discussions on different topics to this man's house on holidays, when they wanted a change from the usual routine. So this man's kindly, friendly disposition brought its own rewards; not only was he never lonely, but if he ever needed help, there was help forthcoming without even asking for it, even from strangers in strange places. Here the law of karma is dealing, not with actions or words, but with thoughts and attitudes.

The law of karma is interpreted differently in different religions, judging from Jinarajadasa's book entitled First Principles of Theosophy. However, we have given examples from our own observations strictly in relation to the definition that "every action has a reaction equal and opposite". This law is there in all religions but worded differently such as 'you will reap what you sow'.

Among the general laws there are two more which are of significance and those are (1) uniformity stops all growth; that is if everyone had the same salary no matter what their work, wore the same type of clothes, spoke the same language, belonged to the same community, was trained to think alike without questioning, they would reach a plateau beyond which there will be no forward movement. The other law (2) states gigantism leads to extinction. This law has many applications. In fossil record we see that it is the giant animals like dinosaurs and giant plants, like tree ferns, cycads that have become extinct. Apart from physical growth, the law is applicable to political situations too. Throughout history, we see the rise and fall of the all-powerful-dictators like Hitler, Saddam Husain, and terrorist leaders, as well as governments where there was a big gap between the rulers and the ruled as in France in the18th century when the French Revolution took place; and in the 19th century the Russian revolution took place; and in the 20th century there was the breakup of the British Empire.

In every aspect of life there is law and order though in the beginning it may seem haphazard. Dmitri Mendeleyev the designer of the Periodic Table said, "To discover the existence of a general order in nature, and to discover the causes governing this order is the function of science." Mendeleyev's Periodic Table established a clarity that transformed our understanding of chemistry. In the beginning, even when about sixty elements had been identified, no system had been devised to arrange them in any particular order. Mendeleyev who was a Professor of chemistry in the Technical Institute in St Petersburg in Russia in 1864 published a Text Book on Organic Chemistry which was a prize winning text book. In 1869 he wrote another book called The Principles of Chemistry which became a classic work. It was in the course of writing this book that he stumbled on a discovery that led to the establishment of the Periodic Table.

There had been several attempts in the past to organize and classify the elements. Some arranged them according to their properties such as metals, gases etc. Some arranged them according to their atomic weights (i.e. total number of subatomic particles in the atoms of a particular element). In 1866 an English amateur chemist named John Newlands submitted a paper to the Chemical Society arranging the elements based on atomic weights. He had noticed that every 8th element had properties similar to the 1st element in the group. So he concluded that elements were multiples of 8 like the notes in an octave. So he named his system The Law of Octaves. But his idea was greeted with mockery because none of them realized that Newland had come very close to discovering a useful table of elements. Mendeleyev did not know about this when he was writing his book on The Principles of Chemistry. As he worked on his book he wondered if there might be a relationship between atomic weights and properties of elements. He noticed a pattern emerging as he arranged the elements in groups of seven. He saw that the properties periodically repeated themselves and that is how The Periodic Table eventually got its name. He arranged the elements in horizontal rows called periods and vertical columns called groups. The elements were arranged from left to right in ascending order of atomic weights. In the columns reading from up to down the elements were grouped with similar valences and properties such as metals and gases for example. Mendeleyev's system also did not get immediate acceptance. Its importance became apparent only as time moved on. The Table had gaps, but Mendeleyev had predicted that these would be filled with elements yet to be discovered, and he was proved right. This won Mendeleyev international renown. Today the Periodic Table contains 90 naturally occurring elements and 24 others that have been created in laboratories.

The father of chemistry however is Antoine Lavoisier as he was the first one to suggest that every substance can exist in three states, that is, solid, liquid, and gas, and that air has mass, and is made up of two main elements oxygen and nitrogen, and also that water is a compound of two elements hydrogen and oxygen. Lavoisier was a meticulous experimenter and championed the idea of exact measurements. Lavoisier was not only a scientist, but also a lawyer and social activist. Between the years 1770 and 1780 he prepared a number of reports on different social issues such as food adulteration, improvement of prisons, how glass could be made better, whether canal water could be drunk, and how water could be stored aboard ships, as well as a number of other issues, and made many genuine improvements in social conditions.

Carl Linnaeus was a botanist from Sweden who brought out the law and order that exists in the plant world today. In the seventh century, Botanists and Zoologists in Europe were beginning to be aware of the incredible diversity in natural life, and getting confused at the teeming range of variations. Gradually as they worked on it, a pattern began to emerge. The variations that they observed, was not an interminable process of variation. There were breaks and discontinuities in the diversities. It then became clear that these plants could be divided into groups, and there were obvious differences between the groups which were based mainly on structure adjusted to suit a given environment. In the course of evolution, natural selection had favored those which have a combination of features most advantages to their particular habitat and way of life. For instance angiosperms is a very broad group of plants containing trees, shrubs, herbs, and vines, which bear flowers with sepals, petals, stamens, and pistils, members of which are adapted to live in the tropics as well as the temperate climes and occur widely throughout the world, while gymnosperms which are mostly trees with no flowers and have only cones, have a restricted occurrence. Then there are other broad groups like mosses, ferns, lichens, algae, fungi, none of which bear any flowers, and are relatively much smaller in size, and are adapted to different habitats. It was also observed that members of any one group have more in common with one another, than members of other groups. Further, when features and properties of every individual within a group are studied they can be divided into smaller groups forming families, and each family into a number of genera, and each genus into a number of species. This basic process is known as classification and the purpose of it is, identification of the species, which are the empirical units of classification.

The part of systemic Botany that gives names to plants is known as nomenclature, for which a set of rules have been drawn up. It is known as International code of Botanical Nomenclature (I C B N). The fundamental provision of this code is that the scientific plant names should be in Latin, which was chosen because it was a dead language and thus avoids any element of national bias. The name of a species is made up of two parts. First comes the name of the genus followed by the species name for example *Pinus roxburghi* written in italics with the first letter of the genus name in capital, but all the letters of the species in small case. The name when written is followed by the name of the person who first discovered and described and named the plant. This system was first established by Linnaeus. Classification of animals is also more or less on the same lines.

Most people have no notion of the vastness of space, and the mysteriously ordered universe in which we live. Also they do not understand the significance of the theories put forward by great Thinkers, and proved by painstaking experiments, observations, analyses, and interpretation by the Scientists. Neither do they understand the far reaching effects these efforts have upon the evolution of the human soul. Most of all, they do not connect up these findings with the awakening of awareness of the hidden power that lies dormant within each individual. They at the most consider these advances in science as a means of comfort and freedom from drudgery.

THE OBJECTIVE OF LIFE AND ITS IMPACT ON HUMANS

I N the past, humans have wondered about the fundamental principles and fundamental facts of their being what they are, and the world they live in being what it is, and where all these came from, and when it all began. They have also stood in fear and awe of the unseen power that holds and moves all the heavenly bodies in their prescribed courses, and seem to have a control over all living Beings as well. Gradually the findings of Copernicus, Galileo, Newton, and others have paved the way for us towards a better understanding than hitherto, of the world we live in.

Discoveries of Planck and Einstein, Lamarck and Darwin, have then moved us from the world of perception that have dominated our understanding of the universe until then, to the world of the unseen, and the great laws underlying the workings of the interior spiritual thought forces, and aroused our awareness to the divine sequence running throughout the universe in space and time, and pervading all life-forms from the minutest to the most complex life-form of the humans, taking each life-form one step at a time forward at its own pace. According to Ralph Waldo Trine everything is worked out in the unseen before it is manifested in the 'seen'. In his book entitled 'In Tune with the Infinite' he states "The realm of the unseen is the realm of the cause. The realm of the 'seen' is the realm of the effect. The nature of the effect is always determined and conditioned by the nature of the cause."

The moment we fully realize who and what we are, and our relationship to the life-forms around us, the difference between life and life-forms, the difference between abstract and concrete, the difference between soul and body and the role played by both in an individual's evolution, the difference between positive and negative traits and what they do to us, as demonstrated continually by the law of karma, and finally the objective and process of creating life-forms, and the nature and role of death in the scheme of things, then we begin to understand the true objective of life, and the work plan by which the objective is achieved.

Since the time of Darwin we have mistaken the objective of life, to be a fight for survival. In the plant and animal kingdoms the fight for survival involves fight for space and food and mates. In humans it is a fight for wealth and power. Since we believe that all that can possibly be achieved must be achieved in the current life time, 'for we live only once' there is a scramble to reach the pinnacle of power and wealth and recognition, no matter by what means we achieve it, and no matter what harm we do to others, or what destruction we cause. In the process we don't realize the harm we cause to ourselves. We germinate and nurture all the evil spirits of egoism, arrogance, selfishness, and insensitivity in our aura, and soon become a slave to them; and since all negative traits are self destructive, they fill us with fear, worry, and despair of not being able to live up to the expectations of others to win their admiration, and gain popularity. So there is no forward or upward movement in our self development. Furthermore, we are mere slaves to the evil spirits in our aura, as well as to the public in general. So we lose our self respect and self esteem, and soon it shows up in our personality because we become touchy, petulant, irritable, angry, and resentful.

On the other hand, when we keep the law of karma in the forefront of our mind we begin to build our own world following God's guidance, and have full faith in Him that whatever He does is for our own growth, and our development into a full positive force. According to Ralph Waldo Trine nothing negative can ever enter into our lives unless it finds therein something corresponding to itself which makes it possible. He states "No evil or undesirable condition of any kind can come into our lives, unless there is already in them that which invites it, and so makes it possible for it to come. The sooner we begin to look within ourselves for the cause of whatever comes to us, the better it will be, for so much the sooner will we begin to make conditions within ourselves, such that only good may enter." In order to help us look for the cause within ourselves we have to remember that according to the law of karma, every action has a reaction equal and opposite, and accordingly, every individual makes his or her own destiny (that is the syllabus of experiences) for every coming reincarnation, by his or her own desires as well as karma.

When we open ourselves to this sustaining power of reasoning, we will then feel more in control of ourselves, and be free from fear, and therefore free from the weakening corroding power of worry. We will realize that whatever is happening to us is a reflection of our own actions, which we have to correct straight away, in order to get things back on track. If it is some financial loss that we are incurring, it may be that the law of karma is alerting us to something we have overlooked in the deal, or if it is something which is beyond our control, we have to realize that it is a debt we have incurred either sometime in this life time, or some previous incarnations, and the sooner we pay it off the better it is, for we will be free of a burden; and pay it off we will have to, as there is no escape from it. So there is no point in getting resentful and revengeful, for that would mean that we have not learnt the lessons which that particular experience had to teach us. In such situations, there is a repetition in our lives of the same situation with some variations, for now although the debt has been paid, the lesson attached to it has not been learnt. On the other hand, if we face the situation with dignity and equanimity, and feel no anger, resentment, or revengefulness, and only become aware of how the law of karma works, and our faith in God remains, and we know that He will find a solution to our predicament, then He will open new doors of opportunities for us to go forward. If we are filled with fear and worry which are the two evil spirits that carry the germs of despair, we will indeed be defeated.

What the world needs now is an efficient, harmonious, and cooperative life backed by a basic understanding of all subjects, which is absolutely necessary for a life of creative power and therefore of use to all. We have to keep in mind at all times that the objective of life is to increase our consciousness to gain awareness, knowledge, wisdom, and sensitivity, to prepare us for the final day of judgment, as these are the qualities that would be required for us to enter the kingdom of heaven, and live as spirits and work with God to increase the positive force and decrease the negative force. As life is a neutral force made up of both positive and negative forces, it will be possible only to decrease the negative force but not to eliminate it altogether. This is done by increasing the positive force and maintaining a given ratio.

All are individual expressions of the one life, though some are dominated by the positive force and some by the negative force, depending on the inherent traits present in the energy when the first unit of life was created. But the aim of life is to move away from the negative force and move towards the positive force. As we open ourselves fully to the realization of this, and develop self control and germinate and nurture the seeds of the positive force, and dry up the seeds of the negative force present in our aura, we bring harmony to our individual lives; and out of that harmony we create a world of harmony and cooperation, in which each individual and each community enjoys the fruits of their own karma. Thus we enjoy freedom from prejudices, hatred, arrogance, and double standards, and prevent ourselves from being enslaved and disrupted by evil spirits of negative traits, which we in our folly, nurture and strengthen in our aura, causing eventual self destruction, and so cause the destruction of humanity as a whole.

Success or failure in any venture depends on the attitude of the people concerned. Attitude is governed by two main traits and those are (1) courage which is a positive creative type of thought, and (2) fear which is a negative self destructive type of thought. Both positive and negative thoughts are silent conversations which we hold with our inner self - the aura, in which reside the good spirits on one side and the evil spirits on the other. This really is a reflection of life itself which has both good and evil in latent form. The only difference in the two situations is that, whereas in unexpressed life, the two traits are in latent form, in life-forms they are in the active manifested form, depending on which of the two traits have been and nourished and grown into spirits.

Thoughts are forces subtle and vital which is either continually building and shaping our lives or dragging us to despair and destruction. Positive thoughts engender strength from within, that is, the support from the good spirits who dwell within us, and attract help and support from without. On the other hand evil thoughts of fear, worry, and despair strengthen the evil spirits within us and weaken and enslave us and fill us with a sense of hopelessness.

Whereas courage begets success, fear begets failure. If we have faith, hope, and courage, within us we cannot fail. Courage actually means absolute faith in God, and faith means that only what God gives us is worth having; and hope means that God will be beside us to open our minds to the lessons we have to learn from the results of the follies we have made; and once we have learnt those lessons, God will open new doors for us. However we have to be able to discern between the courage to do the right thing, and the bravado of a terrorist who sacrifices his own life for a cause which brings destruction and sorrow. When we understand the difference between *courage and bravado,* then we understand the difference between positive energy and negative energy.

It is only when we are ignorant about cosmic laws that we feel that we can get away from the results of our karma (thought word and action). So if we know that causing pain and loss for others, in however small or big measure, it will come back to us in equal measure, we will be more aware of the consequences of our own actions, and not only actions but thoughts and words too. The functioning of the law of karma is evidence to the fact that God does not punish anyone; He only tries to save Wrong Doers from getting into the clutches of the devil and be enslaved. The law of karma does not deal with punishments. It is merely a corrective measure to make people aware of the effect of their actions, and develop some sensitivity in them, by showing them a reflection of their own actions. The law of karma is a unique method of maintaining justice without punishments.

According to Ralph Waldo Trine, 'through the law of karma each individual is building his or her own world. By building from within we attract from without. Thoughts are the forces by which like builds like, and like attracts like, and everything is first worked out in the unseen before it is manifested in the seen'. The things to aim for in life, is to continually grow emotionally, spiritually, intellectually, physiologically, psychologically, financially, and socially. By doing so, we will be germinating and nurturing the latent good within us to manifest themselves as good spirits in our aura.

According to Antony Robbins "the power to magically transform our lives into our greatest dream lies waiting within us all." But what lies within us to 'magically transform our lives' depends on the extent of our inner strength which can overcome all temptations. Any person who is self indulgent and undisciplined will first have to strive hard to build that inner strength. It is only then that we can transform ourselves.

The word 'power' however means different things to different people. For some, power is the ability to direct one's own thought processes, one's own behavior patterns, and conquer one's own negative qualities, by drying up the seeds of negative traits in one's aura, and thus produce the precise results required. Some see power as a means to control others, and a life without power they feel is a colorless life. Some people feel that power is a corrupting factor and therefore to be avoided. It is very few people who think of power as an inner strength which helps them to stand up for Truth and Justice, to resist temptations, and to hold themselves back from being revengeful and judgmental. Yet the power supported by an inner strength is by far the most powerful. All other types of power such as power of wealth, status, popularity, and leadership are all ephemeral. It is the inner strength alone which enables us to draw on the power of God which we can do only when we are in tune with God.

Today the most important and powerful people are those with specialized knowledge, because we are now living in the Information Age. The Industrial Age that revolutionized life styles has merged with the Communication Age, where newer and newer inventions are coming up almost every month. Whereas in the beginning, people had to depend on books, journals, magazines, and newspapers available mostly in libraries, now all that information and more are available at every one's doorstep through the internet. But with all this access to information, most people don't seem to connect up things, and see their significance. For example, everyone knows that we all have seperate and distinct biological identities in the form of D N A Yet the general belief is that we have only this one life to live after which we will be in the grave till the last judgment day. If that is the case what would be the purpose of having separate and distinct identities? Yet the general belief is that we have only one life to live, then what would be the purpose of having separate identities for each individual, and a judgment day, if there is only one lifetime and the identity is going to be annulled by the individual's death. The fact that we have an identification mark may be regarded as proof that we have to pass through several reincarnations which involve repeated life times, and different forms, for which it is necessary to have an identity which cannot be destroyed but develops through different incarnations This is of course speculation based on the assumption that nothing appears suddenly, and has to develop gradually.

Though most people have overlooked their spiritual development, and the objective of life, but have muddled along without any purpose or direction, yet they have directed their attention to acquiring the latest scientific inventions which have enabled them to live a life of constant stimulation of the brain. And in the process, they have increased their awareness, and knowledge.   This sort of a situation gets them into a neurophysiologic state. If they are people with positive attitudes of love, joy, confidence, and belief in their own ability, (all of which come out of their inner strength), they benefit from the situation. But if their outlook is negative, and they allow themselves to be commanded by the evil spirits in their aura, then they are in a state of confusion, irritation, anger, anxiety, sadness, and frustration because of unhealthy competition It is such people who have to take themselves in hand without any delay, and overpower all these evil spirits, by adopting the most important attitude of all, and that is self control.

Understanding the different phases we pass through, and watching our own thoughts and our reactions to them, is the best way to increase our awareness. But people who switch off their minds to escape an unpleasant situation, or worse still look for the cause of that situation as something brought about by others, gradually decrease their awareness, and develop double standards which paralyze their perception of things. From time immemorial mankind has tried different ways of altering the states of their mind by different means such as with rituals of different kinds, hypnosis, chanting, drugs, sex, foods of different kinds, fasting, music etc.

We perceive all our experiences in life through our five senses, that is (1) vision (sight), (2) audition (hearing), (3) olfaction (smell), (4) gestation(taste) and (5)kinesthesia (feeling). But we mostly use three of these and those are visual, auditory, and kinesthetic systems to make decisions that affect our behavior patterns. Each of these specialized receptors transmits external stimuli to the brain, which then takes these electrical signals and filters them into an internal representation. This is the mechanism by which we perceive the world in our thoughts and represent it to the outside. This mechanism is affected by our physiology, that is, by what we eat, how we breathe, our posture, our muscle tension, and the overall level of the biochemical reactions of our bodies. So to change our attitude to life involves a whole series of chemical reactions. A person who is very alert and attentive is normally physically vibrant and perceives the world in a different way, from a person who is tired and sick and feeling down in the dumps. Therefore, to improve our attitude to life we have to overhaul our whole system starting with the mind. As there is a great variation from person to person in all the factors mentioned above, we see that each person undergoes a given experience in a different way. Further, the level of consciousness of each person varies in his or her capacity to use the different signals being sent out by the environment; and the brain in its capacity to filter and store the information it needs. Our perceptions are also modeled greatly by the books we read, the people we interact with, and the profession we follow, and the everyday sights we see, and the sounds we hear. If a person lives or works with people who are judgmental, and continually find faults with everything and everyone, that person is living in a world of negative vibrations. The consequence is, that the person starts making certain generalizations about himself or herself, and soon starts believing them, and these ideas will govern and direct all actions in the future, of the person.

However all thoughts, words, actions, behavior patterns, and states of mind, are all controlled by the good or evil spirits residing in our aura. We are responsible to have germinated and nurtured them from their latent state to their manifested forms, through our own attitudes to the different experiences we have had to go through in life. We have used the terms, 'reincarnation' and 'karma' which are also found in Hindu literature. But our interpretations differ completely from those found in the Hindu literature, both about reincarnation as well as the law of karma. Our representations are based entirely on our scientific observations and interpretations of our observations. For instance it is an undisputed belief that life evolved from single celled organisms and the belief is substantiated by fossil records as well as scientific observations, like when the nucleus which contains all the genetic material is removed from a living cell it lives and functions for a period of time. This is an indication that in the beginning the prokaryotic unicellular Being, which had no genetic material, lived and survived for a period of time only. But as the energy within the prokaryotic Cellular Being increased in consciousness and awareness of the potentials of its own body it separated out a tiny molecule of nucleoprotein to act as a gene, to take charge of the development of structure, growth, and multiplication of the unicellular Being.

In Hindu literature, although they mention different life-forms starting from the simplest to the most complex, they regard all of them as a manifestation of God without any particular purpose. They do not speak about increasing consciousness, awareness, knowledge and wisdom being responsible for increasing complexity of the life-forms. Also they do not speak about life having positive and negative forces, and the aim of life being to separate the positive from the negative. They only mention the universal soul which they term as Paramathma, and the individual soul which they term as jivatma. Also they don't mention life as having any specific objective.

Another point is about our interpretation of reincarnation, as a change in form in an organism with the passage of time, without the involvement of chromosomes. This is based on our observation of the different changes in forms that a group of organisms undergo at different stages of growth, including in the humans. This is not a Hindu concept, for they consider reincarnation of only humans, and that even only after death, and they do mention about group souls of the plant and animal kingdom getting individualized and migrating into human bodies.

They do not mention how this can happen. So presumably it is just speculation without any particular basis.

Regarding reincarnation after death of an organism, we regard death as a separation of the energy from the body, and the combining of that energy with a larger molecule of matter to develop into a higher life-form. This process is repeated from one reincarnation to the other; with each reincarnation developing into a more and more complex life-form which is brought about by increase in consciousness and awareness of the energy that pervades the body of the life-form. This goes on till it reaches the stage where there is differentiation of sexes in the plant kingdom as well as the animal kingdom. From then on reproduction takes place by the union of the sexes. According to us, reincarnation is the visible result of increased consciousness in the energy which pervades the whole body of different groups of life-forms. Observations from the history of evolution of life-forms have shown us, that when a given life-form has reached a stage, beyond which there cannot be any further forward or upward movement of the energy which pervades its body, because of the limitations in the form, then that form becomes extinct. This statement is based on the fact that the human form has arrived on the scene only after the extinction of the Dinosaurs. Also in the human form there does not seem to be many changes in the physical traits with the passage of time. The changes are directed more towards mental development.

The above observation is our own, and differs radically from the Hindu concept where reincarnation is described in various ways, such as transmigration of souls, and souls picking up an astral body and mental body, and dwelling in them for a period of time after death. This is supposed to happen somewhere in a place called astral world, and mental world. This is explained by Jinarajadasa in his book entitled 'The First Principles of Theosophy' but it is not very clear how a soul can pick up readymade bodies to dwell in. The scientific observation is that nothing comes readymade. In the reincarnation that we refer to, the soul after separation from the body combines with a molecule of matter in the same way as the sperm combines with the ovum, and has to undergo a whole series of development processes before a body develops. This development process is repeated in every incarnation, and that happens in this world, and not as in the Hindu concept in some vague astral world. It is observed that in every life-form there is a repetition of its entire evolutionary history in the gestation period. So there is a great deal of difference between our interpretation of reincarnation and that of the Hindu concept.

Our interpretation of the law of karma is based on our observation of the law which states that every action has a reaction equal and opposite. We feel that it is applicable equally to all, whether children or grownups, male or female, old or young, Believers or Nonbelievers. In very simple cases, the effect is immediate as already explained earlier, but in more complicated cases the effect gets delayed especially if it involves more than one person and more than one place. Each action, thought or word seems to have individual effects. The law of karma is first and foremost a corrective measure to make people aware of the implications of their own actions, by reversing the situations and showing them a mirror image of their own actions.

In the Hindu concept as presented by Jinarajadasa in his book entitled 'The First Principles of Theosophy' the law of karma differs completely from our views. According to him the law of karma is applicable differently to different levels of people."For the adepts, disciples, and the chosen ones of the Master, suitable adjustments are made to the sum total of their karma, so as to enable them to have a better destiny than what it would be, if the law was strictly applied". Another point of difference is that we have observed the law is applicable as individual cases, but in the Hindu concept the sum total of a person's actions has to be considered instead of considering each action separately.

BIBLIOGRAPHY

Altenburg, E. (1973) Genetics

Brady, J . (1979) Biological clocks

Brunton, P. (1974) The Inner Reality

Burnett, L. (1950) The Universe and Dr Einstein

Cherayil, J.D. (1971) Gene and the Genetic code

Clarke, R. W. (1971) Einstein —The Life and Times

Farndon,J. ,Woolf, A. (2005) The great scientists of the world

Rooney, A. ,Gogerly, L From Euclid to Stephan Hawking

Gardener, M. (1070) Great essays in science

Hesslop-Harrison (1978) Cellular Recognition system

Huxley, J. S. (1932) The Stream of Life

Jinarajadasa (1929) The First Principles of Theosophy

Keith, A. (1932) Concerning Mans Origin

Lipton, B.C. (2010) Biology of Beliefs

McElroy , W.D.(1969) Cell Physiology and Biochemistry

Readers Digest (2008) Our Mysterious Universe

Robbins, A. (1986) Unlimited Power

Trine, R. W. (1952) In Tune with the Infinite

Appendix 1 - Geological Periods

ERA	PERIOD	TOP LAYER
CENOZOIC ERA	QUARTERNARY	ABOUT 1.5 MILLION YEARS AGO
	TERTIARY	65 MILLION YEARS AGO
MESOZOIC ERA	CRETACEOUS	135 MILLION YEARS AGO
	JURASSIC	190 MILLION YEARS AGO
	TRIASSIC	225 MILLION YEARS AGO
	PERMIAN	280 MILLION YEARS AGO
	CARBONIFEROUS	345 MILLION YEARS AGO
PALAEOZOIC ERA	DEVONIAN	395 MILLION YEARS AGO
	SILURIAN	440 MILLION YEARS AGO
	ORDOVICIAN	500 MILLION YEARS AGO
		570 MILLION YEARS AGO
PRECAMBRIAN ERA	CAMBRIAN	600 MILLION YEARS AGO
	PRECAMBRIAN	

Appendix 2A - Simplified Classification of Plant Kingdom

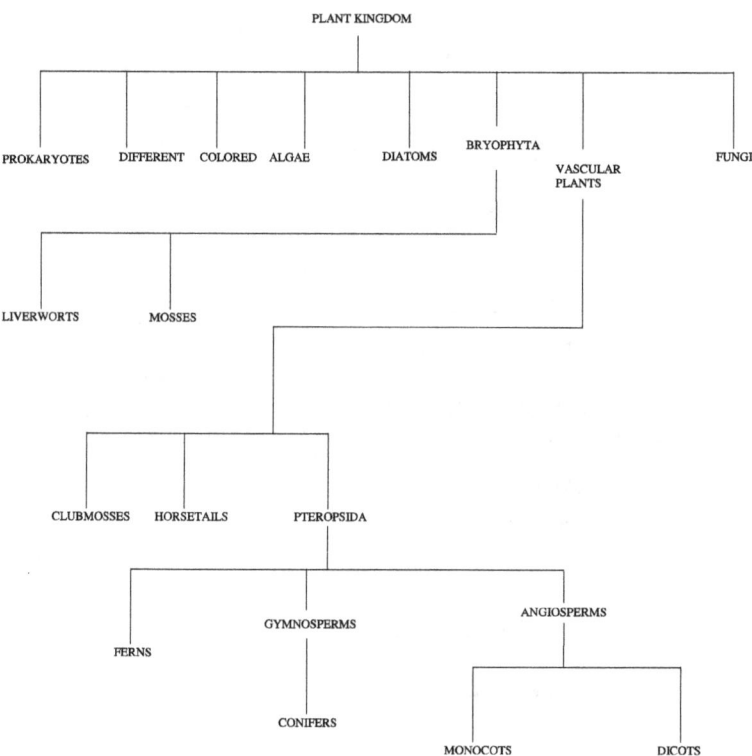

Appendix 2B - Simplified Classification of Animal Kingdom

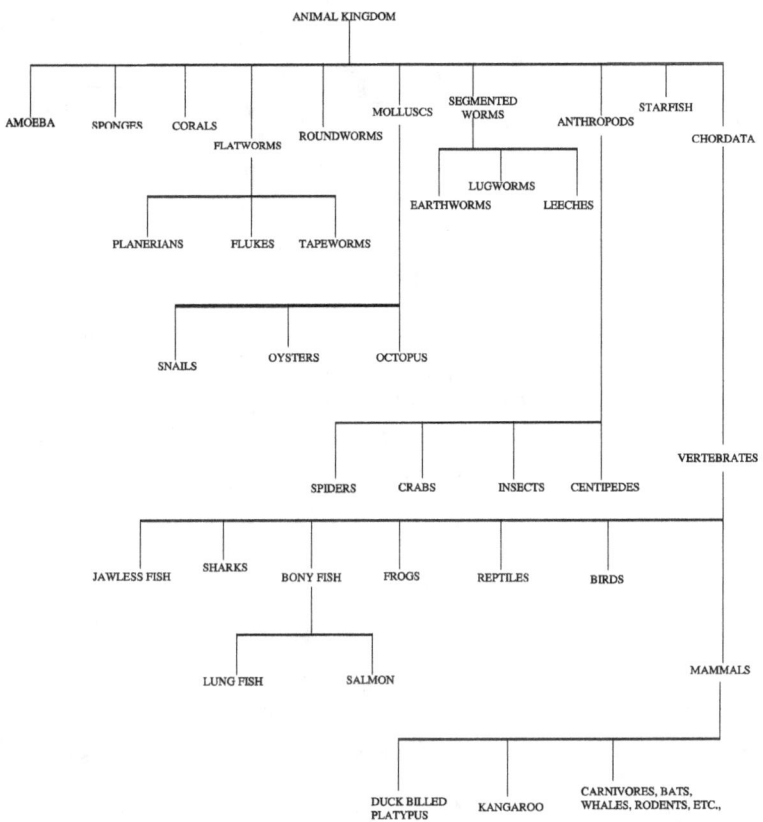

Appendix 3 - Continental Drift

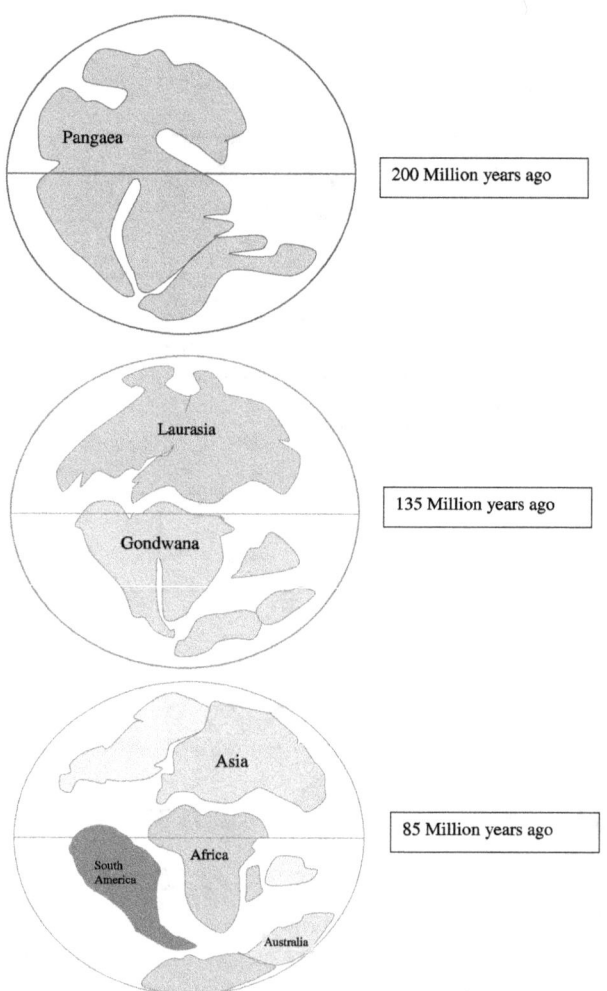

Appendix 4 - Difference Between Plant & Animal Cell Systems

PLANT CELL SYSTEM

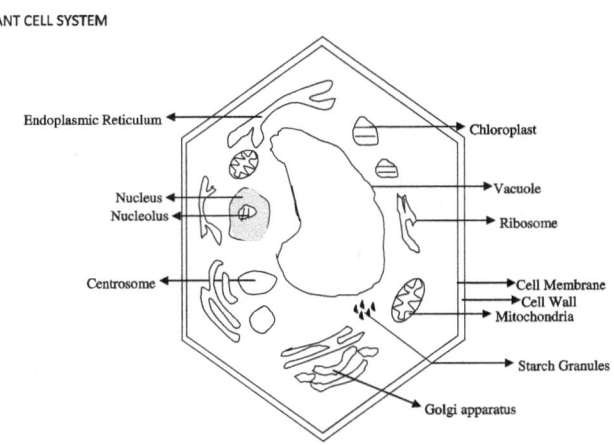

ANIMAL CELL SYSTEM

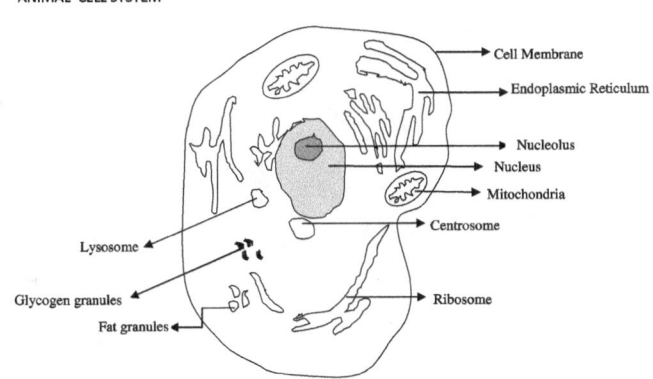

Appendix 5 - DNA & RNA

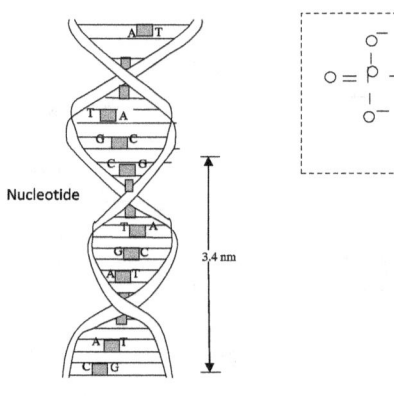

Nucleotide

3.4 nm

DNA Double Helix

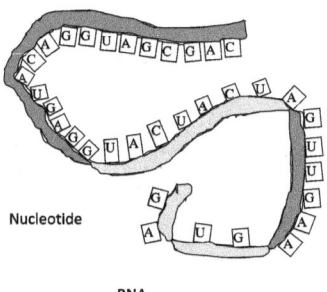

Nucleotide

RNA